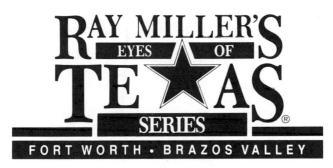

RAY MILLER'S
EYES OF TEXAS
TE★AS
SERIES
FORT WORTH • BRAZOS VALLEY

SECOND EDITION

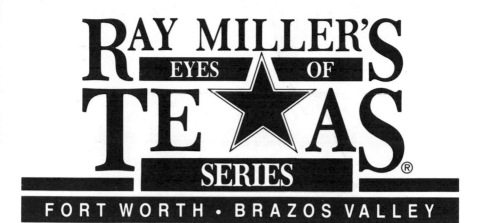

RAY MILLER'S
EYES ★ OF
TE★AS
SERIES
FORT WORTH · BRAZOS VALLEY

SECOND EDITION

Gulf Publishing Company
Houston, Texas

Ray Miller's
Eyes of Texas® Series
Fort Worth • Brazos Valley
Second Edition

Gulf Publishing Company
Book Division
P.O. Box 2608, Houston, Texas 77252-2608

10 9 8 7 6 5 4 3 2 1

Library of Congress Cataloging-in-Publication Data

Miller, Ray, 1919–
    [Eyes of Texas series. Fort Worth/Brazos Valley]
    Ray Miller's Eyes of Texas series. Fort Worth/Brazos Valley.—2nd ed.
        p. cm.
    The [x] in Texas in the title appears as a star.
    Rev. ed. of: The Eyes of Texas travel guide. 1978.
    Includes index.
    ISBN 0-88415-016-X.—ISBN 0-88415-005-4 (pbk.)
    1. Brazos River Valley (Tex.)—Description and travel—Guidebooks. 2. Fort Worth Region (Tex.)—Description and travel—Guidebooks. 3. Brazos River Valley (Tex.)—History, Local. 4. Fort Worth Region (Tex.)—History. Local. I. Miller, Ray, 1919– Eyes of Texas travel guide.
F392.B842M55 1991
976.4′1—dc20   91-20596
                                                          CIP

Contents

1. The Austin Colony Area, 1

2. Waco and Central Texas, 69

Gulf books bring you the best of Texas:

Ray Miller's *Eyes of Texas*® Historical Guides:

Austin/Hill Country/West Texas,
  2nd Edition

Dallas/East Texas, 2nd Edition

Fort Worth/Brazos Valley,
  2nd Edition

Houston/Gulf Coast, 2nd Edition

San Antonio/Border, 2nd Edition

Panhandle/Plains

Ray Miller's *Galveston*, 2nd Edition

Ray Miller's *Houston*, 2nd Edition

Ray Miller's *Texas Forts*

Ray Miller's *Texas Parks*

Backroads of Texas

A Guide to Fishing in Texas

Guide to Texas Rivers and Streams

Hiking and Backpacking Trails of
  Texas, 3rd Edition

Camper's Guide to Texas Parks,
  Lakes, and Forests, 3rd Edition

Beachcomber's Guide to Gulf Coast
  Marine Life, 2nd Edition

Mariner's Atlas Texas Gulf Coast

Birder's Guide to Texas

Why Stop? A Guide to Texas
  Historical Roadside Markers,
  2nd Edition

Bicycling in Texas

Texas Monthly® Field Guides:

Wildflowers, Trees, and Shrubs
  of Texas

Archaeological Sites of Texas

Birds of the Big Bend

Fossils of Texas

Reptiles and Amphibians of Texas

Stone Artifacts of Texas Indians

Texas Snakes

Texas Trees

Wildlife in Texas and the Southwest

Foreword

Texas sprawls over 267,000 square miles, an area larger than most of the world's independent countries.

Rich in history, natural resources, economic opportunity, and natural beauty, Texas is attracting more and more attention as a vacationland and as a pleasant, rewarding place to live and work.

Texas boasts more than a quarter of a million miles of roads, streets, and highways; 624 miles of tidewater coastline; and 91 mountains that are a mile or more high.

The moods and faces of Texas include rugged mountains and sandy seashores, wide plains and majestic forests, some of the nation's great cities and picturesque ghost towns, mighty industrial complexes and small family operated shops.

Ray Miller, in his television programs, has done a commendable job of presenting these facts, of relating history and showcasing the attractions of our state today.

From these programs grew the Eyes of Texas Series, of which this — Fort Worth/Brazos Valley — is the fifth publication.

I have a set of these books in my own library, and I recommend them, and particularly this one, to all who want to become familiar with the many faces of Texas. I think they will help visitors and newcomers understand why Texans, native and adopted, are proud of our state. And they remind us old-timers just how much we have to be proud of.

William P. Clements, Jr.
Governor of Texas
1979-1983
1987-1991

Introduction

This guide covers forty-three counties in the central and north central section of Texas. This area includes the cities of Fort Worth, Wichita Falls, Waco, Temple, Bryan, College Station, and Brenham. It is most of the area drained by the Brazos River.

The Brazos is the longest river in Texas. One branch rises in New Mexico. The Indians called the river Tokonohono. The French explorer LaSalle called it Maligne, after he found out it was not the Mississippi. The Spanish gave the river the name Brazos de Dios. There is some evidence they originally meant the name for the river now called the Colorado. But it was firmly attached to this river by the time the first Anglo settlers came.

There are several stories about why the Spanish chose the name Brazos de Dios for whichever river they gave it to. The English translation is "arms of God." Spanish exploring parties were dying of thirst, in most of the stories, when they stumbled upon the river and hailed it as the answer to their prayers.

Stephen F. Austin could not have chosen a more appropriate place for the first Anglo colony in Texas if he had explored the entire territory, as he did not. Much of the best farmland in Texas is here. Many of the richest cotton plantations were here when cotton was king of the Texas economy. Some of the great cattle empires were founded here. Here ran some of the major cattle trails and the Butterfield Road. Some of the significant clashes between whites and Indians happened here. And so many bright young officers were stationed at the U.S. Army posts here in the 1850s that some people still believe U.S. Secretary of War Jefferson Davis deliberately used the Texas frontier as a training ground for Confederate generals.

Ray Miller
Houston, Texas

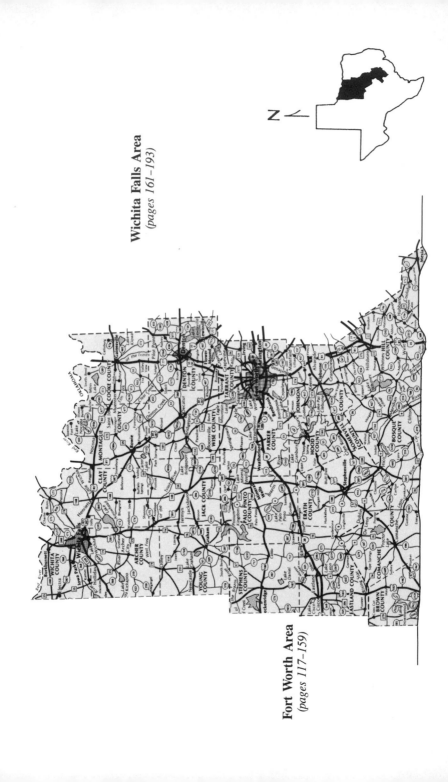

Wichita Falls Area
(pages 161–193)

Fort Worth Area
(pages 117–159)

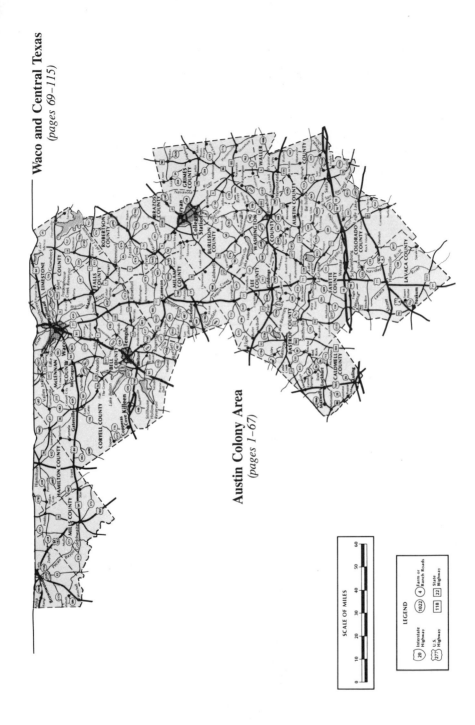

Waco and Central Texas
(pages 69–115)

Austin Colony Area
(pages 1–67)

SCALE OF MILES

0   10   20   30   40   50   60

LEGEND

(20) Interstate Highway   (1022) (4) Farm or Ranch Roads

{277} U.S. Highway   [118] [22] State Highway

The Austin Colony Area

Austin, Colorado, Lavaca, Fayette, Caldwell, Bastrop, Lee, Burleson, Milam, Brazos, Grimes, Waller, and Washington counties.

President Thomas Jefferson made the deal with Napoleon that transferred the Louisiana Territory to the United States in 1803. The only obstacle that then stood between the United States and the Pacific Coast was the territory claimed by Spain, including Texas. U.S. officials had long cherished the notion of extending the boundary of their new republic to the Pacific. The French had claimed, off and on, that the Louisiana Territory included Texas.

So the United States made a tentative effort to claim that Texas was part of what Jefferson had bought. Spain bristled at this and the United States agreed in 1818 that the boundary between U.S. and Spanish territory should be approximately where the line between Louisiana and Texas is now.

Aaron Burr was advocating seizure of some Spanish territory as early as 1796. Burr was working on an invasion plan when President Jefferson had him arrested in 1808. U.S. citizens Philip Nolan, James Long, and Augustus Magee actually made forays into Spanish Texas between 1797 and 1819, and seized and held territory for brief periods. The United States government took no action against them. But Burr was suspected of having designs on some U.S. territory, too.

The Spanish always suspected that the expeditions of Nolan, Long, and Magee actually had the unofficial blessings of the United States government. So it is surprising that the Spanish authorities agreed to let Anglo settlers enter Texas from the United States. But they did in January of 1821, partly in the hope that the Anglo settlements would absorb some of the energies of the Comanche Indians.

A few Anglos had settled earlier in eastern Texas, but most of them had no authority to do so. The sanctioned Anglo settlement of Texas began here in the Brazos Valley. The Texas Declaration of Independence was written and signed here. The government of the Republic of Texas was sitting here when it voted to accept the United States' offer of statehood. If Gonzales was the Lexington of Texas, Washington-on-the-Brazos was our Philadelphia.

Austin County

The father of the man this county was named for came to Texas in 1820 to ask permission to bring some Anglo settlers into Spanish Texas. Moses

1, previous page) Stephen Fuller Austin is often called the father of Texas because he brought the first authorized Anglo settlers here from the United States. He chose this site on the Brazos River to be headquarters for his colony and called the settlement San Felipe de Austin. The bronze statue, on FM 1458, was installed in 1938 and paid for by the Texas Centennial Fund.

2) Stephen F. Austin's desk is one of the exhibits in the Josey General Store Museum at the Stephen F. Austin Historic Site. The museum is in a store building built in the 1840s. There is a small fee for admission to the museum; admission to the Stephen F. Austin Historic Site grounds is free.

3

3) *This may be the oldest government building in Texas. The oldest part was built in 1842 and served as the town hall until the 1970s. The building has also been a school. San Felipe had the first English-language school in Texas. The first real newspaper,* The Telegraph and Texas Register *was originally published in San Felipe. The old town hall is still used for meetings and as a polling place.*

Austin was a native of Connecticut and 59 years old. He had been a prosperous lead mine owner in Missouri. The depression and panic of 1819 had wiped him out and he was looking for a new line of work.

The first Spanish officials Austin talked to about starting an Anglo colony were not very receptive. But a friendly nobleman named Bastrop helped Austin persuade the authorities that an Anglo colony might help them strengthen their tenuous hold on the territory. The Spanish, in January of 1821, authorized Moses Austin to settle 300 immigrant families from the United States on 200,000 acres of land somewhere in Texas. Moses Austin died six months later, leaving his son to carry out the colonization contract.

Stephen F. Austin selected the land that became the original Austin Colony. But Mexico won independence from Spain while the first Austin colonists were moving in, and Stephen F. Austin had to go to Mexico to negotiate a new deal with the new government. He had to make more trips as revolutionary regimes succeeded each other in Mexico City. But Austin was a patient and methodical diplomat. He managed to keep reasonable relations with the various regimes and he eventually obtained additional land grants.

The population of the Austin colonies was around 8,000 by 1832. There were several thousand more Anglos in other colonies by this time. But Austin's colonies were the most successful and Austin had broad authority to regulate affairs in his colonies. He founded the frontier constabulary that became the Texas Rangers. He was a member of the legislature of the Mexican state of Coahuila and Texas.

4

4) *The San Felipe Church was built in the 1830s near the site of the log cabin where the first Texas Sunday school met in 1829. San Felipe still owns much of the land the Mexican government granted for the town site in 1823. The town deeded 600 acres of that land to the state for the Stephen F. Austin State Park in 1940. Residents of San Felipe do not give their town the Spanish pronunciation. They say San FILL-ip.*

Austin's headquarters at San Felipe became the unofficial capital of Anglo Texas and the official headquarters of the San Felipe District the Mexican government established in 1834.

Austin kept his distance from the early advocates of independence from Mexico. He personally helped the Mexicans put down the Fredonian Rebellion in Nacogdoches in 1826. He tried to avoid taking sides in Mexican national politics. But Austin did side with General Antonio Lopez de Santa Anna in 1832. Anastacio Bustamante was president at the time and Santa Anna was trying to depose him. Santa Anna succeeded and became president. Texans had believed Santa Anna's claim that he was for reforms and they started thinking about the kind of reforms they wanted. The series of conventions and consultations that led to the Texas Declaration of Independence started in 1832, at San Felipe.

The Texans' demands initially were for freer immigration laws and separation from Coahuila. Stephen F. Austin continued to believe that reforms could be achieved by peaceful means. In 1834 he was in Mexico City, trying to persuade the national government to grant some of the reforms demanded by the delegates to the Texas Conventions of 1832 and 1833. Santa Anna was provoked by the demands. He had Austin jailed for several months.

Austin did not get back to Texas until the fall of 1835. Fighting between Texans and Mexicans started a short time later at Gonzales. Austin commanded the Texas volunteer army briefly during its march from Gonzales to San Antonio. But the Provisional Government of Texas ordered Austin to go to New Orleans in November of 1835 to negotiate for loans and supplies and he missed the rest of the revolution. Texas was an independent republic when Austin returned in June of 1836.

5

5) *Most services are held in an adjacent newer building, but the original Methodist Church building in Industry is still in good repair. It was built in 1867 and church members did most of the work.*

Austin was nominated for president of the republic but Sam Houston was elected. Houston appointed Austin secretary of state and he was serving in that office when he died December 27, 1836, at Columbia at the age of forty-three. Austin's remains were buried originally on his sister's plantation at Peach Point in Brazoria County, and later moved to the State Cemetery in Austin. The capital city was named for Stephen F. Austin when it was established in 1839. Austin County was named for him when it was established by the first congress of the republic in 1836. The town of San Felipe was the county seat until 1848 when the Austin County government moved to Bellville.

The Convention of 1836 that wrote the Texas Declaration of Independence met at Washington-on-the-Brazos in what is now Washington County. But San Felipe was the site of the Convention of 1832, where Anglo settlers first petitioned for reforms and separation from Coahuila. The Convention of 1833 met at San Felipe to draft the proposed constitution for the proposed separate state of Texas that Stephen F. Austin carried to Mexico City in 1834. And the Consultation of 1835 met at San Felipe to establish the Provisional Government of Texas, which started the serious preparations for the revolution.

San Felipe was abandoned and burned in the spring of 1836 when Sam Houston and the Texas Army were retreating eastward. Sam Houston had taken command of the Texas Army at Gonzales after the Mexicans sacked the Alamo. The retreating Texans reached San Felipe on March 28th. Houston detailed a small force commanded by Mosley Baker to guard the Brazos River crossing at San Felipe while the main Texas force moved upriver to the Groce plantation. Santa Anna and his Mexicans reached San Felipe on April 7th. The river was in flood and there was Baker's force to be dealt with, so the Mexican commander-in-chief decided to cross the river somewhere else. He

6) Industry was the first German settlement in Texas. The Industry post office opened in this building in 1838. It was the first post office west of Galveston.

left San Felipe on April 9th and marched south to Fort Bend where he crossed the Brazos on April 12th and headed for San Jacinto, where he probably ever after wished he never had gone.

Captain Baker's troops burned everything that would burn before they left San Felipe. Baker always claimed Houston had left him orders to burn the town. Houston always claimed he had not. Many of Houston's actions at this stage of the revolution were loudly criticized. Some Texans claimed Houston actually had no intention of fighting the Mexicans. They claimed that when Houston eventually turned his army to the south to confront Santa Anna it was because his troops had made it plain they would follow him nowhere else. Houston never told anybody what his intentions were and so when he achieved his remarkable victory at San Jacinto, no one could prove he did not plan it.

The town of San Felipe was rebuilt after the war but it never again was as important as it had been before. The population of San Felipe now is about 400. The population of Austin County reached 20,000 in 1900 and then started declining as people moved from farms to the cities. The population started increasing again in the 1970s. Sealy, on I-10, is now the biggest town in the county.

7

7) *German immigrants established the community of Cat Spring in 1844. Robert Justus Kleberg was one of the original settlers. His son married Alice King and became head of the King Ranch. The Cat Spring meeting hall was built by the Cat Spring Agricultural Society, organized in 1856.*

8

8) *The roads around Nelsonville are favorites with sightseers in the spring when the wildflowers are out.*

Cotton was the chief crop here in Stephen F. Austin's time and for a long time after that. Some of the first cotton gins in Texas were in Austin County. But now most of Texas' cotton is grown on the plains of West Texas, and livestock and feed grains are more important here. The first oil discovery in Austin County was at Raccoon Bend in 1928.

Park — San Felipe

Stephen F. Austin State Historical Park, off FM 1458. Golf course, swimming, camping. Fee.

Colorado County

This county, too, was part of the original Stephen F. Austin Colony. The Spanish explorer Martin de Alarcon had traveled through what is now Colorado County as early as 1689, but the Spanish had never attempted any settlement in the area.

Moses Austin's benefactor, Baron de Bastrop, apparently helped Stephen F. Austin choose the land for his first colony. Some accounts say Bastrop in

9

10

9) The tree died years ago but Colorado County has savved the trunk because it was under this tree that the first session of court in Colorado County was held, in 1837.
10) The present Colorado County Courthouse in Columbus was built in 1909. It was restored in the early 1980s.

8

11

11) An old water tower on the courthouse square now houses the United Daughters of the Confederacy Museum. Open third weekend in May and by appointment. Free.

1823 personally assisted Austin in surveying a site on the Colorado River as a possible location for the colony's headquarters. The site was near where the old Atascocita Road crossed the Colorado. There reputedly had been an Indian village at the site at some earlier time.

Austin eventually decided to locate his headquarters at San Felipe on the Brazos. But a village developed, anyway, at the site he had considered on the Colorado. The settlement was called Beason's, or Beason's Crossing, because Benjamin Beason was operating a ferry at the crossing. The name was changed to Columbus, for the city in Ohio, in 1835. Columbus claimed to be the first Anglo town ever platted in Texas, on the basis of that 1823 survey.

The Texas Army burned Columbus during its retreat from Gonzales after the fall of the Alamo in March of 1836. The Texas Army actually crossed the Colorado at Burnam's Ferry, north of Columbus, and marched down the east bank of the river to a spot opposite Columbus. A Mexican army led by General Ramirez y Sesma camped a few miles west of Columbus on March 18th. General Santa Anna and more Mexican troops reached this camp March 25th. Many of the Texans wanted to fight. But General Sam Houston decided to continue the retreat. He had the ferryboats at Beason's and Burnam's destroyed and set fire to Columbus.

Most of the residents of Columbus fled when the Texas Army left. They returned after the Texas triumph at San Jacinto on April 21st, 1836. They rebuilt their town and the town prospered. The congress of the republic created

9

12   13

12) Dr. Charles Tait built this home at 526 Wallace Street in 1856. The Taits also had a large plantation outside town. This place is still known as the Tait town house.

13) The Magnolia Homes Tour of Columbus owns this house on Walnut Street between Bowie and Live Oak. It has been added onto since, but the original section was built about 1860. This is known as the Senftenburg-Brandon house. It is open every year during the Magnolia Homes Tour the third weekend in May and tours can also be arranged by appointment. P.O. Box 817, Columbus, TX 78934. Free.

14) The Colorado River has laid down huge beds of gravel over the centuries. Gravel is hauled from here to road jobs and building sites all over southeast Texas. Some goes by train; some in tractor-trailer rigs capable of carrying 25 tons.

14

Colorado County in the fall of 1836 and Columbus was designated the county seat. Judge R. M. Williamson presided over the first court session in Columbus, before the first courthouse was built. Judge Williamson held court under a tree that has been known ever since as the Court Oak.

One of the first houses built after the settlers returned to Columbus still survives. Abram and Nancy Alley built their cabin on their property outside Columbus in the summer of 1836. Their descendants later had the cabin moved to Columbus and turned it over to the Magnolia Homes Tour, Incorporated. The Homes Tour was organized in 1961 to encourage preservation

15

15) Frelsburg was founded in north-eastern Colorado County in 1834 by William Frels. He donated the land for the Trinity Lutheran Church.

16

16) Helen and Bill Farris operate the 1912 hotel they have restored in Eagle Lake. Many of the customers are goose hunters. Wild birds are attracted to this area by the water and rice fields. The biggest wildflower seed farm in Texas is nearby and open to visitors. (Directions available from Eagle Lake Chamber of Commerce.) Eagle Lake was so named by the Indians, supposedly because a Karankawa maiden had a habit of sending her suitors across the natural lake here to fetch young eagles for her.

17) *The Attwater Prairie Chicken National Refuge in Colorado County is open to the public from sunrise to sunset every day. The entrance to the refuge is off FM 3013, ten miles south of Sealy. The best time to see the endangered native grouse is between the first of February and the end of April.*

17

18

18) *This was the San Jacinto Hotel, in Weimar, when people were traveling by train. It's been reborn as the Weimar Country Inn for the bed and breakfast trade, and also serves lunch and dinner.*

and restoration of old buildings in Columbus. The organization conducts a tour of the city's historic buildings each year, in May.

One of the real showplaces of old Columbus failed to survive. A Scotsman named Robert Robson came here in 1839 and built a castle on the bank of the Colorado. The place had a moat and a drawbridge. There was a garden on the roof and Robson probably was the first settler in Texas to have water piped into his home. The parties the Scotsman conducted in his castle were the talk of the frontier. But Robson had not chosen his building site as cannily as he might have. A flood washed out the river bank in 1869 and undermined the castle so badly that it had to be demolished. A meat and ice company built a plant on the site in 1883 and it is gone, now, too.

Several people were killed in a family feud in Colorado County in the early days. The trouble started when two members of the Stafford ranching family were shot to death outside a saloon in Columbus in 1888. The Staffords blamed members of the Townsend ranching family for the attack and retaliated. Staffords and Townsends continued to kill each other occasionally until 1906.

Cotton was the chief crop here in the early days and it often went to the coast on river steamers. Several paddlewheelers stopped regularly at Columbus and one of them came to grief on a sandbar nearby in the late 1850s. The engine of the *Moccasin Belle* was salvaged and moved to the Charles Tait plantation to power a sawmill. The old steamer's anchor became an ornament on the lawn of the Tait townhouse in Columbus.

Livestock and feed grains are more important than cotton in Colorado County today. The county has several oil and gas fields and major deposits of sand and gravel.

Museum — Columbus

Koliba Home Museum, 1124 Front St. 10 am to 6 pm daily. Fee.

Lavaca County

The Spanish never seriously disturbed the Indian residents of what is now Lavaca County during the years they ruled Texas. But they did know the area. The Atascocita Road between Goliad and Liberty passed through the southeastern corner of what is now Lavaca County and La Bahia Road between Goliad and Nacogdoches passed through the northwestern corner. The early Spanish explorers named the two rivers that drain the county: Lavaca is Spanish for "the cow" and probably referred to the buffaloes the Spanish found here; Navidad is Spanish for "nativity."

In the 1820s, the Lavaca River was the boundary between Stephen F. Austin's colony and the colonial grant the government of Mexico awarded in 1825 to Green C. DeWitt. Austin had settled 12 Anglo families in this area by 1831, and DeWitt had 21 families living here. Cotton was the principal crop in the beginning. A settler named William Milligan built the first gin and the Milligan gin became a meeting place for settlers plotting separation from Mexico.

Lavaca County was not actually organized until 1846, after Texas joined the United States. It was formed from parts of Victoria, Gonzales, Jackson, and Colorado counties.

A settlement called Petersburg was the original county seat, but Petersburg no longer exists. The government and the population moved to Hallettsville in 1852. John Hallett started the settlement of Hallettsville in 1833. His widow later donated land for a town site. The residents then decided their settlement should be the county seat and they forced an election. The announced result was a majority in favor of moving the government from Petersburg to Hal-

19) *The government of Lavaca County has occupied five different buildings since the county was organized in 1846. The fifth one is holding up well. The present courthouse in Hallettsville was built in 1897. It is listed in the* National Register of Historic places.

19

20

20) *The former home of Dr. James Lay is the most unusual house in Hallettsville. A French man named Victor Hugo designed it, in the 1860s. Hugo had been a diplomat in Mexico. He fled to Texas when the Mexicans executed the Emperor Maximilian. Dr. Lay took him in and befriended him and Hugo designed this house to return the favor.*

14

21) *It's never made the big time, but the Spoetzl Brewery has been making beer in Shiner for a long time. The brewery was started by local businessmen in 1909. They sold it to German immigrant Cosmos Spoetzl in 1914. The plant has changed hands several times since, but the product is still called Shiner beer. A hospitality room serves samples.*

21

lettsville. The people of Petersburg demanded a recount. But somebody destroyed the ballots before the recount could be accomplished. A district court ruled that the decision in favor of Hallettsville had to stand. The people of Petersburg refused for a time to let the county records be moved. Eventually the people of Hallettsville organized a posse of about 200 men to go get the records. Hallettsville has been the county seat ever since.

The first courthouse was built in Hallettsville in 1852. It was abandoned in 1890 and the government did business in Riemenschneider's Furniture Store until the present courthouse was completed in 1897.

The first railroad reached Lavaca County in 1887. The San Antonio and Aransas Pass Railroad created the town of Yoakum, on the boundary between Lavaca and DeWitt County. Yoakum was named for railroad man B. F. Yoakum. He later had a large role in developing the citrus industry in the Rio Grande Valley. The town of Yoakum is noted chiefly for tomatoes and leather goods.

The San Antonio and Aransas Pass Railroad also provided the inspiration for the town of Shiner. This town was named for settler H. B. Shiner because he donated the land for the town site when the rail line came through. Shiner is the marketing center for an area populated mostly by German and Czech farmers. The first residents of Shiner came here from a community that had been known as Half Moon, a little farther west. The rail line missed their town. They just closed the town and moved to the rail line.

The San Antonio and Aransas Pass Railroad caused at least one other Lavaca County community to relocate. Moulton originally was two miles northwest of where it is now. The rail line missed the original town site and

22) *The house William and India Green built in 1853 has a historical marker, but very little care. The Green property is now part of the Green-Dickson Boy Scout Campground. It is off US 90A west of Shiner.*

23) *The oldest business building in the present town of Moulton is being remodeled to house the local bank. The Boehm Building was built in 1908.*

24) *Seven years older is the building Sam and Will Moore built to house their school. This building is now part of the Moulton Independent School complex.*

22

23

24

the residents moved to the rail line. Moulton probably was named for early settler E. L. Moulton. The San Antonio and Aransas Pass Railroad was absorbed into the Southern Pacific system in 1925.

Farmers in Lavaca County grow feed grains, rice, pecans, and peaches, but cattle, hogs, and poultry account for most of the agricultural income. The county has several small oil fields.

Museums — Shiner

Edwin Wolters Museum, 306 South Ave. I. By appointment. Donations.
Spoetzl Brewery Museum, Monday and Tuesday mornings, Thursday and Friday afternoons, 11 am to 3 pm Saturday. Free.

Fayette County

Spear and arrow points found chiefly around Winchester indicate that Indians inhabited the area that is now Fayette County at least ten or twelve thousand years ago.

This area was included in the Stephen F. Austin colony but at least a couple of Anglos settled here before the Austin colony was established. Aylett C. Buckner and Peter Powell had no official permission to do so, but they settled in 1819 at the junction of Buckner's Creek and the Colorado River near the site of the present city of La Grange. Buckner and Powell were soldiers of fortune. They came to Texas first with the Guiterrez-Magee Expedition in 1812 and came back again with Dr. James Long in 1819. Several of Long's followers, besides Buckner and Powell stayed in Texas after Long was captured and killed by the Mexicans in 1822. They were the original illegal aliens in Texas.

Stephen F. Austin made land grants to Buckner and Powell and these grants gave them the status of legitimate colonists. Buckner was killed in one of the

25

25) The remains of some local heroes killed in encounters with the Mexicans were buried in 1848 on this bluff overlooking the Colorado and the city of La Grange. Some of the men were killed in the Battle of Salado in 1842. The others were captured and executed after they took part in an unsuccessful attack on the Mexican border town of Mier. The Daughters of the Republic of Texas bought the site in 1905 and gave it to the state. The state put up the monument in 1936, created a small park, and named it Monument Hill. US 77 just south of La Grange.

26

26) Monument Hill is adjacent to the site where H. L. Kreische established a quarry in the 1830s. Kreische built a brewery in the quarry in the 1860s and he was building a large house when he was killed in an accident. The state has acquired the site, stabilized the ruins of the brewery, and added it to the park. Fee.

colonists' early skirmishes with the Mexicans at Velasco in 1832. Buckner and Powell had settled on the Colorado River where the Bahia Road crossed. It was a logical place for a settlement when Austin's colonists began moving in. John Henry Moore started a ferry service at the crossing in 1831. The settlement was surveyed, platted, and named La Grange when Fayette County was created in 1837 from parts of Bastrop and Colorado counties.

Some historians believe the county was named for a county in Tennessee. Some others believe it was named for the Marquis de Lafayette because of the assistance he gave the American colonists in the Revolutionary War. Subscribers to the latter theory say the city of La Grange was named for Lafayette's estate, but it could also have been named for a city in Tennessee.

William Rabb was the first Austin colonist to get a land grant in what is now Fayette County. He built the first grist mill, in 1831, on Rabb's Creek.

The colonists in what is now Fayette County were always quick to respond to calls for help from other settlers. John Moore recruited a force of volunteers here in the fall of 1835 to help the settlers at Gonzales resist the Mexican army's efforts to recover a cannon the Mexicans had lent to the settlers. Moore took command of the Texans at Gonzales and led them in the fight that is

18

27   28

27) *The limestone courthouse in La Grange was built in 1891. This county may have been named for the Marquis de Lafayette, but the residents call it FAY-it County.*

28) *The St. James Episcopal Church was organized in La Grange in 1855. The present building at Monroe and Colorado was built in 1885. It is in the* National Register of Historic Places.

29) *The Stuermer General Store at Ledbetter has been owned by the same family since 1891. It is also a short-order cafe.*

30) *The little lake the Lower Colorado River Authority and the city of Austin created to provide cooling water for a power plant on Cedar Creek has become a "hot" fishing spot.*

29   30

31) The Texas Department of Agriculture keeps a register of farms and ranches that have been in the same family for more than 100 years. Fayette County has more entries on this register than any other county. The Edgar Roitsches are pictured here on a farm outside La Grange that has been in her family for more than 100 years.

31

32) Little is left of the business district of Muldoon. People still live here, but they do their shopping in Flatonia or La Grange. La Grange is blessed with a Walmart store. Settlement began here in the 1830s. The town was named for Rev. Michael Muldoon. He was the original owner of the land and the Catholic clergyman

32

closest to the early Anglo settlers in Texas. A. B. Kerr's general store opened in this building in 1890. It closed shortly after the end of WWII.

generally regarded as the beginning of the war for independence from Mexico. Moore had come to Texas from Tennessee first in 1818; and he came back to stay in 1821.

Another volunteer force was raised in Fayette County in 1842 to oppose a new Mexican invasion of Texas. Mexican general Adrian Woll had seized San Antonio. Captain Nicholas Mosby Dawson mustered a company of mounted volunteers and rode to Bexar County to join in the fight to oust the invaders. The Fayette County volunteers reached Salado Creek, east of San Antonio, while Woll's Mexicans were doing battle there with a Texas force under Matthew Caldwell. A Mexican cavalry unit spotted Dawson's outfit and surrounded it. Dawson and 34 other Fayette County volunteers were killed. The remains of Dawson and his men were brought back to Fayette County later and buried on Monument Hill, overlooking the city of La Grange. Sam Houston was in his second term as president of the republic at the time. One story is that Houston arranged the ceremony on Monument Hill to make the people of Fayette County feel better about not getting the capitol. The congress of the republic had once voted to put the Texas capitol at the proposed town of Colorado City, across the river from La Grange. Houston had vetoed the bill. It was just as well. The proposed Colorado City site turned out to be subject to serious flooding.

The first Protestant college in Texas opened in 1840 at Rutersville in Fayette County. It was conceived by Methodist missionary Martin Ruter who died two years before the school opened. Ruter College was merged with the Texas Monumental and Military Institute in 1856 and closed when the Civil War began. One of the cadets at the institute when it closed was Sam Houston,

33

33) Many of the residents and most of the businesses moved from High Hill to the new town of Schulenburg on the railroad. Gus Cranz moved his store and built this fancy home at 701 West Avenue in Schulenburg. Lillie Cranz grew up in this house and later married Houston oilman Hugh Roy Cullen. Schulenburg was named for Louis Schulenburg because he donated the land for the town and helped bring the railroad through here in the summer of 1874.

34

34) The little town of Round Top is one of the most thoroughly restored communities in Texas and it is becoming an important cultural center. This is the Community Center in the town square.

35) Settlement began at the community now known as Round Top about 1835. The community had several other names before the present name was adopted. The Bethlehem Lutheran Church here was built in 1866. It has an organ handmade of local cedar wood by early settler John Wantke.

35

36) The Texas Pioneer Arts Foundation was established by the late Charles Bybee and Mrs. Bybee to manage Henkel Square in Round Top. Henkel Square is a collection of restored pioneer buildings with authentic furnishings. Two of the buildings on the property were here from the beginning. The Bybees moved the other buildings in from various locations in the area. Guided tours are available for a fee.

36

37

37) Concert pianist James Dick started a small music school and concert center in 1970 in an abandoned public school building outside Round Top.

38

38) Dick has built his Festival Hill Institute into a major cultural center and showplace with a concert hall he designed himself.

39) The stagecoach inn that the late Ima Hogg restored and presented to the University of Texas is the centerpiece of the Winedale Historic Center on FM 2714 east of Round Top. The center is open to the public on Saturdays and Sundays. Fee.

Jr. Other pioneer educational institutions in Fayette County were the Fayetteville Academy, established in Fayetteville in 1849, and the La Grange Collegiate Institute established the same year in La Grange.

The sporting house alleged in the musical comedy to have been the "Best Little Whorehouse in Texas" was located just off US 71 just east of La Grange until a television crusader from Houston embarrassed officials into closing it. Part of the main building at the old Chicken Ranch was moved to Dallas and turned into a restaurant but the restaurant was not as successful as the original enterprise. It went broke. The building was divided and scattered.

This was plantation country from colonial times until the end of the Civil War. Most of the plantations were divided after the war and sold off to immigrant farmers from Germany and Czechoslovakia.

Fayette County has some oil and gas but livestock and poultry are the biggest factors in the economy today.

Museums

La Grange

N. W. Faison home (1845), 822 US 77 South, Saturday and Sunday afternoons. Fee.

Fayette Heritage Museum and Archives, 855 US 77 South, Daily except Mondays. Free.

Flatonia

E. A. Arnim Archives and Museum, N. Main at SH 95. Sunday afternoons and by appointment. Donations.

40) Praha was called Mulberry by the original Anglo settlers. Czech immigrants changed the name when they came in the 1850s. The Czechs established in Praha the first Czech parochial school in America. They built St. Mary's Church in 1892.

40

Caldwell County

The Spanish explorers Felix de Espinosa, Domingo Ramon, and Pedro de Rivera all came through the area that is now Caldwell County in the early 1700s. The Spanish made no effort to settle the area and they built no missions here. The Lipan Apaches and the Karankawas inhabited the area then. The Comanches had moved in by the time the first Anglo settlers arrived in 1831. The first permanent settlers were Geron and James Hinds.

The Texas legislature created Caldwell County from parts of Bastrop and Gonzales counties in 1848 and named it for Matthew Caldwell. He was born in Kentucky and he lived in Missouri before he came to Texas in 1831. Caldwell was a delegate to the Convention of 1836 and one of the signers of the Texas Declaration of Independence. He was a courier during the revolution. He was a captain of infantry in 1840 when he took part in the Council House Fight in San Antonio and the Plum Creek Fight with the Comanches in what is now Caldwell County. Caldwell was also a member of President Mirabeau Lamar's ill-fated Santa Fe Expedition in 1841. He and most of the other members of that expedition were captured by the Mexicans and imprisoned in Mexico for several months. Caldwell got back to Texas in time to take command of the Texas force that defeated General Adrian Woll's Mexicans

41

41) Nine blocks surrounding the Caldwell County courthouse in Lockhart have been designated a historic district and listed in the National Register of Historic Places. *The courthouse is the centerpiece of the district. It was designed by Alfred Giles and built in 1893.*

42

42) The old Caldwell County Jail is now the Caldwell County Museum, featuring collections of pioneer furnishings, tools, and implements. S. Brazos at E. Market. Wednesday through Sunday, 1 pm to 5 pm, summer months only. The jail was built in 1910.

at the Battle of Salado, outside San Antonio in 1842. Caldwell died in December of that year, six years before this county was created and named for him.

A settlement originally called Plum Creek was designated the county seat. Byrd Lockhart owned most of the settlement so it was renamed for him when it became the seat of the new county government. Byrd Lockhart had come to Texas in 1826 and settled in the Green C. DeWitt Colony. He was awarded the grant at Plum Creek for building roads in the colony. Lockhart was a member of the Texas force that compelled Mexican General Martin Perfecto de Cos to surrender San Antonio and the Alamo in December of 1835.

Lockhart remained at the Alamo until after Mexico's President Antonio Lopez de Santa Anna arrived to take it back. He just missed the fate the other Alamo defenders suffered. Lockhart and Andrew Sowell were sent out to try to round up supplies and reinforcements a couple of days before Santa Anna's Mexicans overwhelmed William Barret Travis and the other defenders on March 6, 1836.

Caldwell County has no large cities. The total population of the county is about 25,000. About a third of the population is concentrated in and around Lockhart. Luling is the second largest city. The Galveston, Harrisburg, and San Antonio Railroad created the town of Luling when it built the first rail line into the county in 1874. Luling was the end of the line for a while. It was a major cattle shipping point and the northern terminus of the wagon road to Chihuahua. It is a fairly quiet place now, but Luling once was known as the toughest town in Texas. It was named for the railroad president's wife.

The Old San Antonio Road between San Antonio and Nacogdoches crossed the northern end of what is now Caldwell County. US 90 runs through Luling but most of the through traffic skirts south of Luling on I-10.

Maxwell was founded in 1880 by Thomas Maxwell. Martindale was established in 1855 by Nancy Martindale. Prairie Lea, founded in 1848, was the home of Prairie Lea Female Institute from 1875 to 1885. The first oil discovery

43) The Clark Library at 217 S. Main in Lockhart was built in 1899. It cost $6,000 and Dr. Eugene Clark provided the money for it in his will. This is said to be the oldest library in continuous use, in Texas.

43

44

44) This marker commemorating the Battle of Plum Creek is in the Lockhart City Park but the battle actually was fought at several other loations in the area. The Texans were using Colt revolvers by the time this battle was fought. Historian T. R. Fehrenback says Ranger Jack Hays was the first Texan to use a Colt in a fight with Indians. That was a year or so before the Plum Creek fight. The Colt gave the rangers their first real advantage over the tough Plains Indians. Ranger Sam Walker helped Sam Colt redesign his original revolver the better to fill the rangers' needs, and the result was the .44 caliber weapon known ever since as the Walker Colt.

27

45

46

47

45) This antique rig in a park in downtown Luling is a memorial to the town's greatest benefactor. Edgar Davis showered money on his employees and his town when he sold the oil field he discovered here in 1922.

46) The Luling Oil Field is still producing. Many of the pumps are within the city limits. The Luling Chamber of Commerce decorates them with characters and caricatures. These are designed, built, and installed by Speedy Thomas.

47) The dam and millrace are still in place, but the old Zedler Mill on the San Marcos River at Luling is falling down. This complex grew from a grist mill established in 1874. Fritz Zedler bought the mill in 1888 and added a cotton gin and a generating plant. The Zedlers at one time were furnishing water and electricity to the city of Luling.

in Caldwell County was made in 1922 near Prairie Lea. Edgar B. Davis drilled the discovery well. He apparently was about the only person persuaded at the time that there might be oil here. Davis was born in Massachusetts. He made fortunes in the shoe business and the rubber business before he came to Texas to look for oil. He drilled six dry holes before he drilled a producer. Davis sold his oil interests in 1926 for 12 million dollars. He gave large bonuses to all his employees. He built a golf course and athletic club for Luling and he endowed the Luling Foundation to conduct research and experiments in soil and water conservation and agricultural procedures.

Some of the first settlers in Caldwell County were planters and cotton was the important crop. Livestock and poultry are more important than crops today but less important than the oil and gas.

Park — Lockhart

Lockhart State Park. US 183 South. Golf course, swimming, camping. Fee.

Bastrop County

Indians of the Tonkawa tribe occupied the area that is now Bastrop County when the first Spanish explorers came through in 1691. The Old Spanish Road, El Camino Real, between San Antonio and the missions on the eastern frontier passed through here and crossed the Colorado River where the city of Bastrop is located now. The Spanish had a small fort at the river crossing around 1800 but they never made any serious attempt to settle the area or challenge the Indians.

The settlement at the river crossing was abandoned and the Tonkawas had been displaced by the Comanches by the time the first Anglos reached what is now Bastrop County about 1825. Part of this area was included in the original Stephen F. Austin Colony and the rest of it was added to the Austin grant in 1827. The first settlers included William Barton, Reuben Hornsby, and Josiah Wilbarger. Barton and Hornsby settled up the river in what is now Travis County. Wilbarger settled where the creek named for him flows into the Colorado River here in Bastrop County. The early settlers here had some

48

48) Bastrop is close enough to Austin to attract commuters and the new citizens have had a lot to do with restoring and preserving old buildings and homes here, including the opera house on Spring Street, built in 1889.

29

49

49) Joseph D. Sayers was a student at Bastrop Military Institute from 1852 'til 1860. Sayers went on to serve in the Confederate Army, the Texas Senate, the U.S. Congress, and the governor's office. Sayers was governor from 1899 to 1903. This house at 1703 Wilson Street was his home.

50

50) The Bastrop County Historical Society has a collection of pioneer artifacts and documents in a museum at 702 Main Street. The oldest part of the museum is a house built in 1850. Saturday and Sunday afternoons. Fee.

51

51) Bastrop County has a new jail. The 1891 jail building adjacent to the courthouse in Bastrop now houses the Chamber of Commerce.

unpleasant experiences with the Comanches. Josiah Wilbarger was wounded and scalped near the present site of Austin in 1833. He survived (and lived for another 12 years) because Mrs. Hornsby found him shortly after the attack and nursed him back to health.

The congress of the republic created Bastrop County in 1836. It originally included all or part of 15 other counties, created later. The original Bastrop County had been known previously as the Municipality of Mina. The Mexicans

52

52) This golf course is part of the Bastrop State Park. There is also a swimming pool in this large park developed by the state and the U.S. Civilian Conservation Corps in the 1930s. Off SH 71 immediately east of Bastrop. Camping. Fee.

53

53) The U.S. Army had a big training base off SH 95 during WWII. Most of Camp Swift is now a National Guard base, but a federal prison and a cancer research center occupy part of the old army camp, too.

gave it that name after Mexico separated from Spain. The Spanish never would have named anything for Francisco Xavier Mina. He was a Spanish rebel and he led one of the attempts to oust the Spanish from Mexico. Mina was captured and executed after he attacked the Spanish garrison at Soto la Marina in Tamaulipas in 1817. The Mexicans declared him a national hero after they succeeded in ousting the Spanish in 1821.

The congress of the Republic of Texas changed the name to Bastrop shortly after it designated the municipality one of the original Texas counties. The name Bastrop honors a benefactor of the early settlers. He said he was Felipe Enrique Neri, Baron de Bastrop. His claims about his origins probably were false but there is no question that he was helpful to the Austins and their colonists. Bastrop had obtained some land grants from the Spanish and he had a business in San Antonio, so he knew his way around. Moses Austin showed up in San Antonio late in 1820 to ask for a land grant and permission to bring in some settlers from the United States. The Spanish authorities were not inclined even to listen to such a proposition. But Moses Austin had the good luck to bump into Bastrop. The baron persuaded the Spanish that their interests might be served by allowing some Anglo settlements to absorb some of the energies of the Comanche Indians the Spanish had never been able to control.

Bastrop served as a translator for Moses Austin and for Moses' son, Stephen F. Austin, after Moses died. Bastrop was representing the Texas colonists in the legislature of the Mexican state of Coahuila and Texas when he died in Saltillo in 1827. The late Texas historian Henderson Shuffler said Bastrop's real name was Philip H. N. Bogel.

The Bastrop Historic District includes 131 buildings. Smithville has a historic district including 23 buildings. Settlement began at Smithville about 1827. The town was named for early settler Frank Smith.

Bastrop and Smithville are about the same size and both are smaller than Elgin, in the north end of the county. Elgin was established when the Houston and Texas Central Railroad came through in 1871. It was named in 1882 for railroad surveyor Robert Elgin. The town had been known between 1871 and 1882 as Glasscock and it was sometimes called Hogeye. Butler and Paige also were established when the Houston and Texas Central came through. McDade is on the rail line but it is older than the railroad. McDade was settled in the early 1840s and named for James W. McDade. Rosanky, in the southeastern corner of the county, was setttled in the 1850s and named for Ed Rosanky.

54

54) One of the historic homes in Smithville is the Burleson house at 207 E. 8th. Murray Burleson once owned most of the land around here. Smithville moved from its original location nearby in 1887 in order to get on the rail line then being built through Bastrop County.

55

55) *The McDade Museum on Main Street in McDade occupies a former saloon built about 1875. The saloon was the scene of a major confrontation between vigilantes and suspected cattle rustlers on Christmas Day in 1883. There was a shoot-out and a lynching and 11 suspected rustlers were dead when it was all over. By appointment.*

56

56) *Abraham Wiley Hill built this house on his plantation at Hill's Prairie in 1854, in the Greek Revival style then prevalent in Texas.*

57

57) Dozens of restored old automobiles crowd the Central Texas Museum of Automotive History at Rosanky. Owner Dick Burdick won the 1989 Great American Car Race in an antique Bentley roadster from his collection. SH 304 south of Bastrop. Weekends only in winter; daily except Monday and Tuesday in summer. Fee.

Many of the early settlers in what is now Bastrop County were planters and the main crop here in the early days was cotton. The first industry was lumbering. There is a large pine forest here, isolated from the East Texas pine belt. The "Lost Pines" extend into western Fayette County. Lumber from this forest was hauled to Austin for the first buildings in the new capital in 1839. There are two state parks in the pine forest now.

Bastrop County has some oil and gas and some lignite. A little cotton is grown here, still. But most of the farm income now comes from livestock and poultry.

Park — Smithville

Buescher State Park. FM 153 off SH 71, northwest of Smithville. Camping. Fee.

Lee County

The area that is now Lee County was inhabited by Indians of the Tonkawa tribe when the first Spanish explorers came in the 1690s. There is no record of any Spanish or Mexican attempt to establish settlements here, but the Old Spanish Road between San Antonio and Nacogdoches came through what is now Lee County. The present SH 21 follows roughly the same route: through Manheim, Lincoln, and Old Dime Box.

The oldest town in Lee County is Lexington, where settlement began about 1848. The town was founded in the early 1850s by James Shaw and named for the town in Massachusetts where the minutemen met the British in 1775.

Some of the earliest settlers in what is now Lee County were Lutheran Wends from Germany. They formed a congregation in Germany with Reverend John Kilian as pastor, and moved in a body to Texas. Six hundred Wends sailed to Galveston in a chartered ship and negotiated the purchase of a league of land. They divided the land into farms, built a church, and established the community of Serbin. The Wends were also the original settlers of Northrup.

The territory now included in Lee County was earlier part of Bastrop, Burleson, Fayette, and Washington counties. The legislature created the present county in 1874 and named it for Confederate hero Robert E. Lee. Serbin had been the most important town in the area before 1871. But the Houston and Texas Central Railroad changed that when it laid its line from Houston to Austin several miles to the north of Serbin. A new town was established on the rail line and named for Brenham banker J. D. Giddings. Most of the businesses in Serbin moved to Giddings and the new town was designated the county seat when Lee County was organized.

J. D. Giddings settled in Washington County in 1838. He organized the first bank in Brenham and promoted the first railroad to serve that town. It was a short line connecting with the Houston and Texas Central at Hempstead. Giddings became a stockholder in the Houston and Texas Central when that line absorbed his, and this made him eligible to have a railroad town named for him. The Lee County seat is that town.

 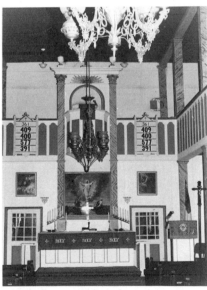

58   59

58) Five hundred Wends came to what is now Lee County from Germany in 1854 and established the town of Serbin. They built St. Paul's Lutheran Church in 1871. Services were conducted originally in Wendish and German.

59) The Wends wanted to have the highest pulpit in Texas. It is on the second level, above the altar, eleven feet above floor level. The pews, the light fixtures, and the feather painting on the columns in St. Paul's all are original.

60

61

60) *Bill Longley grew up in Lee County and took up gunslinging at an early age. He was 27 and had been blamed for 32 killings when he was sentenced to be hanged in Giddings in 1878.*

61) *History records that Bill Longley was hanged October 11, 1878, and his name is on this marker in the Giddings cemetery. But some people believe the hanging was a fake.*

62

62) *Tax reveues rose substantially in Lee County during the oil boom in the early 1980s. The county government invested part of the windfall in the restoration of the brick and limestone courthouse in Giddings. This building was designed by J. R. Gordon and built in 1899. Gordon also designed the courthouses at Decatur, Waxahachie, and New Braunfels.*

The first Lee County courthouse was built in Giddings in 1878. The same year, the county's most notorious outlaw was hanged. The outlaw was William Preston Longley, usually called Wild Bill Longley. He was one of the genuine badmen of the early West. Longley was born into a respectable family in Austin County in 1851. The family moved to what is now Lee County two years later, and Bill grew up near the present community of Lincoln. He killed three men in this vicinity before he was 20. He left for a while after that. He came back again and was soon accused of stealing cattle. A band of vigilantes tried to hang Bill, but he survived and moved away again. He moved around Missouri, Wyoming, and various parts of Texas, was blamed for several more killings, and sentenced to prison for murder. Longley escaped from prison and was blamed for several more killings before he moved back to Lee County in 1877. He killed another man, and fled to Louisiana where he was captured. He was returned to Giddings, tried, and sentenced to death. He had been blamed by this time for 32 killings.

The hanging was conducted in public in Giddings on October 11, 1878. But there is a persistent legend that Longley made arrangements with the sheriff to rig himself up in a harness that permitted him to survive the hanging. This legend has Wild Bill living out his life in Louisiana under an assumed name and dying a natural death in 1923.

Cotton was once the biggest money maker in Lee County. Livestock and poultry account for most of the agricultural income now, but minerals are the biggest factor in the economy of the county. Oil was discovered in northern Lee County in 1939. There is also some gas and some lignite.

Museums

Lexington

Pioneer Village Museum. Daily except Sunday. Free.

63

63) The Texas Department of Agriculture maintains a seed lab at Giddings. The seed labs experiment with various grasses and check and verify the quality and labelling of seeds offered for sale in the state.

Serbin

Texas Wendish Heritage Museum. Daily 1 to 5 pm except Sunday.

Parks — Dime Box

Nails Creek Division of Lake Somerville, off FM 180. Camping. Fee.

*64) The town of Dime Box was origi-
nally called Brown's Mill. The carrier
hauling the mail to and from Giddings
had a lot of requests to do errands in
Giddings for the people on his route.
Carrier John Ratliff charged a dime for
each errand and put up a box where
the customers could leave their instruc-
tions and their dimes. This inspired the
town to adopt the name Dime Box. The
town moved two miles in 1913 to a new
location on the Texas and New Orleans
Railroad. Not much has happened
since.*

64

Burleson County

The Old San Antonio Road, El Camino Real of Spanish colonial days, came through what is now Burleson County at an angle from southwest to northeast, following the approximate route of the present SH 21 through the present city of Caldwell. The Spanish may have tried a little farming here as early as the 1700s.

The southern two thirds of what is now Burleson County was included in the original grant to Stephen F. Austin. The northern third was part of the grant made originally to Robert Leftwich in 1825, later to become known as the Robertson Colony. Some of the history of the Robertson Colony is included in the chapter on Robertson County.

The first Anglo settlers started moving in here about 1825. The independent spirit of the colonists from the United States worried the Mexican authorities and the Mexican congress decided in 1830 to put a stop to immigration from the United States. Many of the immigrants were coming in by way of the Camino Real. The Mexicans established a fort where the Camino Real crossed the Brazos River, to enforce the ban on immigration.

The ban was not easy to enforce. Stephen F. Austin persuaded the Mexican authorities to exempt his colonists, so the ban never was complete. And the chief enforcer here was not strong for enforcement. Jose Francisco Ruiz was the commandant at Fort Tenoxtitlan. He had been a big supporter of the

65

65) *The present Burleson County was one of the places the Mexican government established a fort during its attempt to restrict immigration from the United States in the early 1830s.*

66

66) *The commander of Fort Tenoxtitlan did not agree with the attempt to restrict immigration. Jose Ruiz reported to Mexico City that the restrictions were unenforceable. The fort was abandoned. Ruiz stayed in Texas and eventually joined the advocates of Texas independence.*

67

67) *The home of the late Caldwell mayor Thomas Kraitcher, Jr., on Buck Street, has been restored and furnished by the Burleson County Historical Society. It is open for tours and lunch on Fridays.*

68

68) *Somerville is an important railroad junction. The Santa Fe gives its cross ties their creosote treatment here.*

39

69) *The Army Corps of Engineers maintains five parks around Lake Somerville. The Birch Creek Unit of the Somerville State Park also is in Burleson County, on Park Road 57, west of Lyons. Camping. Fee.*

69

70) *Some Aggies make regular trips from College Station to Snook to stock up on kolaches at the Snook Baking Company. Proprietor Lydia Faust wins prizes with her kolaches. People in Snook know kolaches. The town was settled by Czechs.*

70

campaign to free Mexico from Spanish rule but he had little sympathy with the Mexican regimes that succeeded the Spanish viceroys. Ruiz became friendly with the Anglo colonists. He sent word back to his superiors that the ban on immigration was unenforceable. Ruiz eventually joined the colonists in their revolt against Mexican rule. He was a delegate to the Convention of 1836 that wrote the Texas Declaration of Independence. He and Jose Antonio Navarro of San Antonio were the only native Texans to sign the declaration. Only a marker remains where Fort Tenoxtitlan stood, about 14 miles northeast of Caldwell. There has been some talk of building a replica.

Part of the present Burleson County was included within the boundaries of Milam County when it was established by the first congress of the republic in 1836. The town of Caldwell was the county seat of Milam County until the legislature in 1846 decided to create a new county from parts of Burleson

County and Washington County. The new county was named for San Jacinto veteran and Indian fighter Edward Burleson. He was a signer of the Texas Declaration of Independence, a member of congress during the days of the republic, and vice president during Sam Houston's second term as president of Texas. Caldwell was designated county seat of Burleson County when it was organized. Settlement began at Caldwell in the 1840s. The town was named for Matthew Caldwell. He came to Texas from Kentucky by way of Missouri in 1831, signed the Texas Declaration of Independence, and served as a courier in the revolution.

Snook, in southeastern Burleson County, was settled by Czech immigrants in the 1880s and called Sebesta's Corner until 1895, when it was renamed for settler John Snook.

Lyons, in southern Burleson County, started as a work camp during construction of the Gulf, Colorado, and Santa Fe Railroad in 1878. It was named for W. A. Lyon because he donated the town site.

Somerville also got its start during construction of the Gulf, Colorado, and Santa Fe. Two branches of the line joined here. The first settlers moved in about 1883. The town was named for railroad president Albert Somerville.

Deanville was a shipping point on the Houston and Texas Central Railroad in the 1880s and '90s, but Deanville is older than the railroads. It was established in plantation days and named for planter Jim Dean.

Cotton was the important crop here before the Civil War, but most of the land is devoted now to raising livestock and poultry. Oil and gas are major factors in the economy.

71) The old Spanish road between Nacogdoches and San Antonio crossed Burleson County on approximately the same route as the present SH 21.

71

Museums

Caldwell

Burleson County Museum (courthouse). Fridays and by appointment. Free.

Somerville

Somerville Historical Museum, SH 36 at 8th St. Saturday and Sunday.

Milam County _____

This is one of the areas where the Spanish tried to convert and educate the Indians. The Indians who lived here when the Spanish came were members of the Coco, Mayeye, Orcoquiza, and Karankawa tribes. The Franciscans established three missions along the San Gabriel River. The earliest Spanish explorers had named this river for San Francisco Xavier and the missions San Francisco Xavier de Horcasitas, Neustra Senora de la Candelaria, and San Ildefonso were known, after they were established in 1748, as the San Xavier missions. The three missions were protected by the Presidio San Francisco Xavier, commanded by Felipe Rabago y Teran. He and the missionaries evidently did not get along well together. One of the Franciscans was murdered.

72) This county was named for Ben Milam and a statue of Milam stands on the courthouse grounds in Cameron. Milam was leading the Texas assault on the Mexican garrison in San Antonio when he was killed in December of 1835.

72

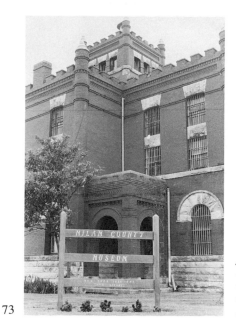

73

73) The county has a new jail. The old jail built across the street from the courthouse in 1895 now houses the Milam County Museum. Daily except Sunday and Monday, 9 am to noon and 1 pm to 5 pm. Donations invited.

Teran was suspected of being involved and the bad feelings that grew from this undermined the whole endeavor. The missions were abandoned in 1755. Little evidence of them remains.

The present Milam County was part of a vast area the Mexican government granted in 1825 to the Texas Association of Nashville, Tennessee. This grant was known originally as the Leftwich Grant because Robert Leftwich handled the association's negotiations with the Mexicans. Association members Sterling and Felix Robertson were the most active in exploring and developing the grant, and the colony became known as the Robertson Colony. The official Mexican designation was Municipality of Viesca. A little settlement called Nashville, on the west bank of the Brazos, was administrative headquarters for the Robertson Colony. Nashville was near the present US 79 crossing.

Texas settlers changed the name of the Robertson Colony from Municipality of Viesca to Municipality of Milam during the Consultation of 1835. The Consultation was held after fighting started between Mexicans and Texans at Gonzales, but before the Texans seized San Antonio and the Alamo. Delegates decided at the Consultation not to try to separate Texas from Mexico. But they decided in favor of trying to get Mexico to let Texas be separated from Coahuila. The name the delegates chose for the municipality survives as the name of this county. It honors Ben Milam, a native of Kentucky who showed up in Texas first as an Indian trader in 1818. Milam took part in some of the early efforts to oust the Spanish from Texas and Mexico and he was granted Mexican citizenship when Mexico won independence. He took up the cause

74) *The original County Home Demonstration Agent in Texas was Edna Westbrook Trigg of Milam County. The concept and the job evolved from work Mrs. Trigg began doing with farm girls here in 1911.*

74

75

75) *The John Sosnowys restored this 1895 home just off SH 36 in Cameron. It is open for tours and available for receptions, and right across the street from the Dairy Queen.*

44

76) *The Little River Baptist Church was organized in 1849. The present building was built in 1873. It's on FM 979 east of FM 485.*

of Texas independence in 1835. He was leading the Texan attack on the Alamo on December 5, 1835 when he was killed by a Mexican bullet.

The first congress of the republic made the Municipality of Milam one of the first Texas counties. The legislature took land from the original Milam County since then to create more counties. Land included in the original county now makes up all or part of 24 other counties. The present boundaries of the county were set in 1856. Cameron has been the county seat since 1846. It was named for Ewen Cameron.

Ewen Cameron was born in Scotland. He came to Texas in 1836 to fight in the revolution. Cameron was a member of the Somervell Expedition sent by Sam Houston to raid Mexican border towns in 1842. Cameron was one of the volunteers disinclined to stop the raids when Alexander Somervell called a halt. He and 307 other raiders decided to attack the border town of Mier. They were captured by Mexican troops and marched off toward Mexico City. Cameron and a number of other Texans escaped in February of 1843, but most of them were recaptured. Mexican President Antonio Lopez de Santa Anna ordered them all executed, but the order was modified and one man in ten was to be shot. The 176 recaptured Texans were required to draw beans from a pot containing nine white beans for every black bean. The 17 men drawing black beans were executed and Santa Anna ordered Cameron to be shot, too. He had drawn a white bean but the Mexicans said he had master-minded the escape. Cameron County, in the Lower Valley, was also named for Ewen Cameron. His remains are buried on Monument Hill at La Grange with those of the other slain members of the Mier Expedition.

Rockdale is the home of a large aluminum plant and lignite mine and it is about the same size as Cameron. Thorndale is the third-largest town. Thorndale is in the southwest corner of the county and got its name from the abundance of mesquite and prickly-pear cactus in the area. Buckholts was established

45

77

77) *Texans tried for a long time to make a commercial waterway of the Brazos. Flat-bottomed steamers traveled the river in colonial days. A few locks were built in the early 1900s. They were abandoned because of the floods that occurred regularly before the dams were built. This ruined lock is on the boundary between Milam and Robertson County, at FM 485.*

on the Gulf, Colorado, and Santa Fe Railroad in 1881, and named for John Buckholts because he donated the town site. Milano was established on the International and Great Northern Railroad in 1873 and originally called Milam. Somebody in the Post Office Department evidently made a mistake in copying the name from the application for a post office and the town has been called Milano ever since. Buckholts and Milano have fewer than 500 residents each. Nashville was the county seat from 1836 until 1846 and the principal town in the county. Nashville went into decline when the county seat was moved to Cameron. Nothing is left of it now.

Milam County has some gas and oil in addition to lignite. Livestock and poultry produce more than half the farm income, but substantial crops of cotton, grain, and peanuts are grown here, too.

Brazos County

The Old San Antonio Road of Spanish colonial days crossed the Brazos River on the western edge of what is now Brazos County and crossed the Navasota River at the northern tip of the present county. But neither the Spanish nor the Mexicans ever made a serious attempt at settlement in this area.

78

78) *The Brazos Valley Museum of Natural Science is part of the Brazos County Center at 3232 Briarcrest Drive (FM 1179 East) in Bryan. Thursday through Saturday, 9 am to 5 pm. Sunday, 1 pm to 5 pm. Free.*

79

79) *College Station is the second biggest town in Brazos County (after Bryan) and the biggest thing in College Station is Texas A&M University. One of the dominant buildings on the sprawling campus is the Albritton Tower and Carillon, donated in 1984 by 1943 A&M graduae Ford Albritton, Jr., of Dallas.*

80) A&M was devoted originally to agricultural and mechanical subjects and military science, and all the students were cadets. The university has the biggest agricultural school in the country and the biggest mechanical school, but A&M also excels in a number of technical fields, nuclear science, and space science. The Academic Building in this photograph occupies the site where the original Main Building stood until it was destroyed by fire in 1912. The statue is of Lawrence Sullivan Ross, governor of Texas from 1887 to 1891 and president of A&M from 1891 until he died in 1898.

80

The Spanish gave the Navasota and the Brazos their present names. Earlier explorers had called it by a couple of other names before Pedro de Rivera gave the Navasota its present name in 1727. The Indians reportedly had called it Nabatsoto before the Spanish came. The Indian name for the river we call Brazos was Tokonohono. The full name the Spanish applied to it was Brazos de Dios. This translates to "arms of God," and there are two or three legends concerning the origin of the name but they all have the same theme. A group of Spaniards about to die of thirst discovered the river and named it out of gratitude. There is some evidence that the life-saving river actually was the stream we now know as the Colorado, and that the name Colorado actually was intended for the river we now know as the Brazos. The present names may have resulted from confusion among the early mapmakers but these names were firmly established by the time the first Anglos came.

The area that is now Brazos County was part of the second Stephen F. Austin Colony. Robert Millican settled his family here in 1824. The town of Millican was named for his son Elliott Millican, the first sheriff of Brazos County. Among the other early settlers were James Evetts, Lee Smith, and Mordecai Boon.

Part of what is now Brazos County was included in the original Washington County, along with the present Washington County and parts of the present Burleson and Lee counties. The Mexicans had called this the Municipality of Washington. The first congress of the republic designated it Washington County. The present Brazos County was created in 1841 from parts of Washington and Robertson counties. It was originally given the name Navasota County but the name was changed to Brazos in 1842. The first important towns here were Boonville and Millican. Boonville was named for Mordecai Boon and it was the original county seat, but it died after the county government moved to Bryan in 1866.

Boonville and Millican both were done in by the Houston and Texas Central Railroad, in different ways. The government and the people moved from Boonville to Bryan because Bryan had railroad service and Boonville did not. Millican just happened to be the northern terminus of the railroad for more than five years because that was the point the railroad builders had reached when the Civil War stopped construction in 1861. Millican flourished as a major shipping point but the bubble burst when the Houston and Texas Central began building again, and planter William Joel Bryan donated the site for what became the city of Bryan. The H&TC extended its line to Bryan in 1866, and Bryan was on its way to becoming the principal city in the county.

College Station is the second-biggest city in Brazos County. College Station grew up around the first state college in Texas. The federal government began to make free land available right after the Civil War to states willing to establish schools to teach agricultural and mechanical arts if they also provided courses in military science. The legislature chartered the Agricultural and Mechanical College of Texas in 1871. A&M opened in 1876 with six teachers and 40 students. Jefferson Davis was invited to be the first president of the school. The former president of the Confederacy declined the honor and Thomas Gathright became the first president.

81

81) Membership in the corps of cadets is now optional at A&M and membership is open to women students. Only a small percentage of the students join the corps.

82

82) *A&M's famous Kyle Field has seating for more than 72,000 people. The Aggies have been playing football here since 1911 when the first stands were built. The stands were enlarged in 1929, 1967, and 1979. Kyle Field was named for Edwin Jackson Kyle. He was president of the Athletic Council, 1900-1911, and Dean of the School of Agriculture, 1911-1944.*

83

83) *The Texas Transportation Institute at Texas A&M University has destroyed hundreds of cars in various tests. This institute introduced the crash barrels now widely used on freeways and developed the breakaway sign posts now almost universally used along major highways. The tests are conducted at the old Bryan Air Base.*

84) *The federal government bought the Allen Academy campus in Bryan in 1988 to convert it to a prison for women. Allen Academy used the proceeds from the sale to build a new school on the eastern outskirts of Bryan. R. O. and James Allen established Allen Academy in Madisonville in 1886 and moved it to Bryan in 1896.*

84

Only white male students could attend A&M in the beginning. The restrictions were modified and then lifted entirely in 1970. The legislature changed the name of the school to Texas A&M University in 1963.

A&M furnished more officers for the U.S. armed forces in World War II than any other school in the country. Twenty-thousand Aggies fought in that war. But membership in the corps of cadets is optional at A&M now and most students opt out.

The Bryan Army Air Field, established during World War II to train flight instructors, was closed in 1960 and deeded to Texas A&M in 1962.

Cotton was king here for a hundred years, but there is more ranching than farming in Brazos County today. The county produces significant quantities of oil and gas. There are deposits of lignite, sand, and gravel here, too.

Museum — College Station

Sanders-Metzger Gun Collection, Student Center, Texas A&M Univ. 10 am to 10 pm daily. Free.

Grimes County

The Frenchman responsible for the first Spanish missions and roads in east Texas probably died in what is now Grimes County.

Robert Cavelier, Sieur de la Salle, explored the mouth of the Mississippi River in 1682 and was commissioned by King Louis XIV to create a French settlement there. La Salle and the four shiploads of colonists he brought over landed on the Texas coast, maybe by design but probably by mistake. They lost their ships in a series of mishaps and established a fortified camp on Matagorda Bay. Some of his followers tried to do a little farming and some went with La Salle on various expeditions into the interior. La Salle ostensibly was looking for the Mississippi. The Spanish always believed he was trying

85) There are more bluebonnets in many other places, but the bluebonnets along SH 6 in Grimes County in the spring are more accessible than most and they get a lot of attention. Bluebonnets like well-drained soil so they do best on slopes like this.

to claim their territory for France. No one will ever know what his purpose really was. Some of his followers got provoked with him during one of the expeditions into the interior in 1867 and they killed him. Historians are not unanimous about it, but it is generally believed that La Salle was murdered near the present city of Navasota.

The La Salle intrusion prompted the Spanish to put a lot of effort into shoring up their claim to Texas. They established missions and roads, and one of their early roads crossed the Brazos River about where the Navasota joins it here in the southwest corner of Grimes County. So the Spanish were aware of this area, but they never tried to settle it.

The first settlers here were Anglos brought in by Stephen F. Austin. One of the first was Jared Groce. He was a native of Virginia and he had owned a plantation in Alabama before he migrated to the Brazos Valley in 1821. Groce qualified for a big grant and he bought additional land for the Brazos River plantation he called Bernardo. That plantation was in what is now Waller County. But Groce also built a home in Grimes County near the present city of Navasota. He called it Groce's Retreat because he thought it was a safe distance from the malaria belt in the Brazos bottoms.

The area that is now Grimes County was included first in the original Washington County and then in Montgomery County when Montgomery was split off from Washington County in 1837. The legislature created Grimes County in 1846 and named it for Jesse Grimes. He had settled in this area in 1827. Grimes was one of the signers of the Texas Declaration of Independence. He served in the congress of the republic and in the legislature after Texas joined the United States.

Anderson is no longer the principal town as it was when the county was created. But Anderson is still the county seat. Anderson grew up around one of the first inns to be established in this area. Henry Fanthorp of England came here in 1832 and started a store. He and Mrs. Fanthorp started accommodating guests in their home and it became known as the Fanthorp Inn. The

86

87

86) *The Daughters of the American Revolution and the people of Navasota put up this statue in Navasota in 1930 to honor the French explorer LaSalle. He probably was murdered near this site in 1687 by some of his own men.*

87) *The first stage stop in Grimes County was at the community of Groce's Retreat. That community grew up around the home pioneer planter Jared Groce built at this site on a county road off FM 2, south of the present city of Navasota. Groce also had a large cotton plantation on the Brazos and the first cotton gin in Texas. The gin was near this site.*

88

88) *Roy Weaver and Sons Apiary exports to beekeepers all over the world queen bees raised in the Weaver hives at Lynn Grove. Roy Weaver's grandfather started the bee business here in the 1880s.*

53

89

89) Grimes County has the quaintest courthouse in Texas. It was built in 1891 in Anderson. This town has been the county seat since Grimes County was organized in 1846. Anderson was named for Texas' last vice president, Kenneth L. Anderson.

90

90) Anderson grew up around a stagecoach inn established in 1832 by the Henry Fanthorps. The inn was enlarged several times over the years. The Texas Parks and Wildlife Department bought it in 1977 and restored it and it is now open to the public as a museum.

settlement that grew up around the inn was known for a time as Alta Mira. The name was changed to Anderson after Texas Vice President Kenneth L. Anderson died at the inn in 1845. A school was established in Anderson in 1846 and the population reached 3,000 by 1885. It is less than 400 today.

The principal town in Grimes County now is Navasota, on the river of the same name. The first settler called the place Hollandale because his name was Holland. The settlement was known by a couple of other names before it was named Navasota in 1856.

The Houston and Texas Central Railroad came through Navasota in 1860 and started the little village on its way to becoming the trade center of the area. Anderson didn't get rail service until 1900.

The late country blues musician Mance Lipscomb was born in Grimes County and lived most of his life here. Lipscomb's father was a sharecropper and Mance did farm work almost all of his life. He learned to play the guitar

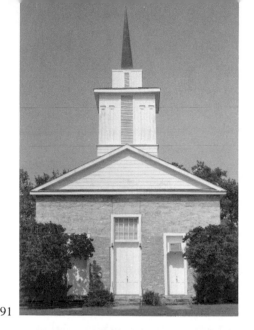

91) *The Baptist church in Anderson was built in 1853. The tower was added in 1855 when Anderson was the most important town in the county.*

91

SARAH BRADLEY
DODSON
1812 — 1848
MADE TEXAS FLAG
SEPT. 1835

92) *Several people designed flags similar to the one Texas finally adopted. The flag Sarah Bradley Dodson designed flew at Washington-on-the-Brazos the day the Declaration of Independence was signed there. Mrs. Dodson is buried in a remote cemetery outside Bedias.*

92

and sing while he was still a boy and he entertained at church socials in this area for years before his style and his original music began to attract attention outside of Texas. Mance Lipscomb enjoyed a few years of popularity but he died here in Grimes County in 1976 at the age of 81 without ever making any real money from his talent.

Cotton was the big money-maker in Grimes County in the early days. There is far more ranching than farming here, now. The county produces some oil and gas and some lignite.

55

Waller County

There was substantial travel through what is now Waller County during Spanish and Mexican times. The Atascocita Road between Goliad and the outposts on the lower Trinity River came through here, but there were no settlements until the Anglos came.

This was part of the Stephen F. Austin Colony. The Mexican government designated it the Municipality of Washington and it became Washington County after the Texas Revolution succeeded in 1836. Washington County was subdivided later and parts of what eventually became Waller County were for a while included in Austin County and Grimes County. Hempstead was designated the county seat when Waller County was created in 1873.

Richard Peebles founded Hempstead when the Houston and Texas Central Railroad came through in 1857. He named his town for one of his relatives. Peebles got the standard land grant for serving in the Texas Army during the revolution and increased his net worth substantially by marrying Mary Ann Groce in 1843. Mrs. Groce was the widow of Jared E. Groce. He was the first rich Anglo in Texas. He brought a herd of livestock, 50 wagonloads of possessions, and 80 or 90 slaves when he moved to the Brazos Valley from Alabama in 1821. He brought cottonseed and raised the first cotton crop in

93

93) The only Groce plantation home still standing is Liendo, built by Leonard Groce in 1853. Liendo was later the home of sculptor Elisabet Ney and her husband. It is outside Hemstead and owned now by the Detering family of Houston.

94 95

94) Norris Wright Cuney was born near Hempstead in 1846. He was one of the first important black political leaders in Texas. Cuney was educated in Pennsylvania and got some legal training in Galveston. He was appointed sergeant-at-arms of the legislature during Reconstruction and he was a power in the Republican Party of Texas until the late 1890s.

95) Prairie View University occupies a site that once was a plantation, six miles south of Hempstead off US 290. This is the John B. Coleman Library building on the Prairie View campus.

Texas. Groce was the original Texas planter. Any cotton farmer with more than 20 slaves was entitled to call himself a planter.

Slavery was a touchy issue while Texas was part of Mexico. The Mexicans abolished slavery when they separated from Spain. They allowed colonists to bring in slaves sometimes, but buying and selling slaves in Texas was illegal and slaves born in Texas were supposed to be freed when they reached the age of 14. The Anglo colonists paid little attention to Mexican laws and slavery became institutionalized when Texas won independence. The constitution of the republic required a slave owner to get the permission of congress before he could free a slave.

Jared Groce qualified for a larger than normal land grant because there were provisions for additional acreage for each slave a colonist brought with him. Groce bought additional land and he and his two sons eventually owned many thousands of acres. Jared Groce built a big house on the east bank of the Brazos near the present city of Hempstead, in 1822. It was the finest house in Texas for a long time. Groce called it Bernardo. The Texas Army camped across the river from Bernardo during its retreat from Gonzales to

96) The Waller County Historical Museum occupies a house built in 1913 by Dr. Paul Donigan. 906 Cooper Street at 5th. Weekdays except Thursdays, 10 am to 2 pm.

San Jacinto. It was at Bernardo that the "Twin Sisters" cannons donated by the citizens of Cincinnati were delivered to Sam Houston.

Jared Groce died in November of 1836. The Bernardo plantation house was destroyed by a flood in 1870 and never rebuilt. Groce's son, Jared III, was installed by that time in his own comfortable plantation home at Pleasant Hill, and Leonard Groce was living stylishly at his Liendo Plantation.

An early Waller County plantation is now a university campus. Jack Kirby developed a plantation on a hill south of Hempstead and called it Prairie View. Kirby's son Jared inherited the place and he and his wife lived in the plantation house until he died in 1865. Mrs. Kirby operated a boarding school in the house for a time. The state bought the property in 1876 and turned it into a school for Negroes. The school was called Prairie View Normal and Industrial College at first. The race restriction was lifted in 1963 but Prairie View A&M University still is attended mostly by black students. The town that grew up around the school is now larger than Hempstead.

Katy is the biggest town in Waller County, but part of Katy is in Harris County and part is in Fort Bend County. Part of Waller is in Harris County. Waller and Waller County both were named for early settler Edwin Waller. He was one of Austin's colonists and one of the signers of the Texas Declaration of Independence. Waller laid out the city of Austin and was the first mayor

97

97) *Waller County is famous for watermelons, and melons are offered for sale at roadside stands all around Hempstead, in the summertime.*

of that city. All of Waller County is included in the Houston Metropolitan Area. Katy and Brookshire have been most affected by Houston's growth because they are closer to Houston and because both are on I-10. Brookshire was named in the 1880s for Texas Army veteran Nathen Brookshire. An earlier settlement at the site had been known as Kellner. Katy was established when the MK&T Railroad came through, and was named for the railroad.

Some of the people of Waller County got wrought up over prohibition in 1905. There was an election and the majority voted to outlaw the sale of liquor. The Prohibitionists called a meeting at Hempstead to petition the governor to send in some rangers to enforce the new law. Opponents of prohibition attended the meeting, too. There was some shouting and pushing and shoving, and then some shooting. Congressman John Pinckney and his brother and two other men were dead when it was over. Two others were wounded. Some people say this was the episode that caused Hempstead to be called "Six Shooter Junction."

Waller County farmers gave up on cotton a long time ago. They grow livestock, rice, soybeans, corn, peanuts, and watermelons. The county has some oil and gas production, and sand and gravel in commercial quantities. Bluebonnets usually make an especially good show around Hempstead in the spring.

Washington County

Indians of the Tamique and Xarame tribes were living here when the Spanish claimed the area and no attempt was made to displace or civilize them. The Spanish Bahia Road passed through what is now Washington County. This road between Goliad and Nacogdoches crossed the Brazos about where the town of Washington-on-the-Brazos is now situated.

Some of the earliest settlers Stephen F. Austin brought to Texas came in on the Bahia Road and crossed the Brazos on rafts they made themselves. Some of these families settled in the vicinity. Andrew Robinson settled his family on the west bank of the Brazos at the site of what was to become Washington-on-the-Brazos. Robinson and his son-in-law John Hall started a ferry service at the river crossing in 1822. Hall and Asa Hoxey and Thomas Gray established the town of Washington-on-the Brazos in 1834. They ar-

98

99

98) *The building where the idea of the Republic of Texas was born did not survive. This replica occupies the site in what is now Washington-on-the-Brazos State Park.*

The Star of the Republic Museum in the park features exhibits depicting various aspects of Texas life. Daily during summer, Wednesday through Sunday during winter months. Free.

99) *Washington-on-the-Brazos was the capital of Texas when Texas joined the union in 1845. The president of the republic at the time was Dr. Anson Jones. This was his house, but it was on another site then. It was moved to the state park in 1936 and restored, and it is open to visitors for a small fee.*

100) *Basil Hatfield built this house in 1853 on his plantation 2½ miles west of Washington-on-the-Brazos, on what is now FM 912. Hatfield owned a store in Washington and operated a steamboat on the Brazos before the railroads came.*

100

101) The Bethlehem Lutheran Church was built at William Penn in the 1890s. It still has a row of hitching posts.

101

ranged for the building where the Convention of 1836 met to declare Texas independent of Mexico. The building was being constructed by settlers Noah Byars and Peter Mercer on speculation. It was not yet finished when the Convention met March 1st, and there were very few accommodations for the convention delegates. But the promoters of Washington-on-the-Brazos paid the rent on the hall and boarded the delegates wherever they could, because they felt the convention would put their town on the map, as it did for a time.

Washington was the first and last capital of the Republic of Texas and it was the county seat of Washington County for a while after the county was created in 1836.

The Interim Government of the Republic left Washington-on-the-Brazos a couple of weeks after the signing of the Texas Declaration of Independence, because Mexican troops were advancing from the west. The Interim Government moved to Harrisburg, to Galveston, to Velsaco, to Columbia, during and after the maneuvers that reached their climax at the Battle of San Jacinto. The first elected government of the republic took office at Columbia and then moved to Houston where it remained during Sam Houston's first term as president. Mirabeau Lamar moved the government to Austin when he succeeded Houston as president in 1839. Sam Houston moved the government back to Houston briefly after he became president again in 1842 and then moved it to Washington-on-the-Brazos. It remained here until Texas joined the United States in 1845, during the administration of President Anson Jones. Austin became the capital again when Texas became a state.

The Mexican government had designated this area the Municipality of Washington in 1835. The first congress of the republic designated it Washington County in 1836. Asa Hoxey supposedly had named the settlement on the Brazos for Washingotn, Georgia, because he once lived there.

The congress of the republic and the legislature took away parts of the original Washington County to create Brazos, Burleson, Lee, Milam, and

61

102) *Baylor University was established in Independence in 1845. The female department was located on the little hill where these columns stand today. Baylor left Independence in 1887.*

102

Navasota counties. The county seat was moved from Washington to Brenham in 1844 because, by that time, Washington was on the edge of what was left of Washington County.

Brenham was named for Richard Fox Brenham. He was one of the less fortunate Texas soldiers of fortune. Brenham got to Texas too late to serve at San Jacinto. But he served briefly in the Texas Army after the revolution ended. He signed up for President Lamar's Santa Fe Expedition and was captured by the Mexicans, along with most of the other members of that expedition. He survived a brief imprisonment and then joined the Somervell Expedition to Laredo and Guerreo. Brenham stayed south of the border to take part in the unauthorized expedition against Mier, where the Mexicans captured him again. They executed him in 1843.

Washington-on-the-Brazos was a river port until about 1860. The port traffic generated enough prosperity to cause residents to think they did not need a railroad. They made no effort to attract the attention of the builders of the Houston and Texas Central Railroad in 1859 when that line was building its pioneer road northward through adjoining Grimes County. But the Brazos was never a satisfactory waterway and the railroad soon put the riverboats out of business. The population of Washington-on-the-Brazos dropped from about 4,000 in 1860 to about 200 in 1885.

Some of the earliest Texas institutions of higher education started in what is now Washington County. The first charter issued by the first congress of the republic for such an institution went to the Independence Academy for Women in 1837. The academy turned co-ed and reached an enrollment of

103

103) Sam and Margaret Houston lived in Independence in the 1850s. Sam was not known for his religious convictions before he married Margaret Lea in 1840. Margaret's people were devout Baptists. Margaret and her mother persuaded Houston to join the Independence Baptist Church.

104

104) The Houstons were living in Huntsville when he died in 1863. Margaret Houston then moved her family to this house in Independence and lived here until she died in 1867. Margaret and her mother both are buried across the street from the Independence Baptist Church. The body of the widow of the premier hero of the Texas Revolution ordinarily would have been buried where he was buried, in Huntsville. But Margaret died of yellow fever. The fever was the mystery scourge of that time and the custom was to bury the victims where they died, as quickly as possible. Mrs. Houston's home was restored in 1984 by Frell Albright and Gene and Frankie Slaughter.

105   106

105) Some of the delegates to the convention that produced the Declaration of Independence down the road at Washington-on-the-Brazos reputedly stayed at the stagecoach inn in Independence. The inn fell down years ago, but Doug Zwiener restored it in 1987.

106) One of the oldest buildings still standing in the Independence area is the home Dr. Asa Hoxey built in 1833. Hoxey came to Texas from Georgia. He owned two large plantations here and he was one of the founders of Washington-on-the-Brazos.

107

107) Mike Shoup has built a thriving business in Independence around roses. He grows rose bushes from cuttings taken from the old roses the early settlers brought to Texas from the Old South.

108

108) The First Christian Church in Brenham was organized in 1877. The present building was built in 1898.

109) Blinn College in Brenham is the oldest county junior college in Texas. Blinn was founded in 1883 by the Southern German Conference of the Methodist Episcopal Church. The original name was Mission Institute. The name was changed to Blinn College in 1889 and it became a county school in 1937. The name Blinn was adopted after a New York family of that name made some substantial contributions to the school.

75 by 1841, but it closed in 1845 and some of its property passed to Baylor University. The Texas Union Baptist Association founded Baylor and named it for Judge Robert E. B. Baylor. He was one of the organizers of the Texas Union Baptist Association and one of the earliest advocates of a Baptist university. The Baylor charter was issued in 1845. The school remained at Independence until 1887 when it was moved to Waco and merged with the Baptists' Waco University.

Robert Emmett Bledsoe Baylor was born in Kentucky in 1793. He was a veteran of the War of 1812. He served in the legislatures of Kentucky and Alabama and represented Alabama in the U.S. Congress before he was ordained in 1839. He was 48 years old when he came to Texas as a missionary and he devoted the rest of his life to the law and his church. Baylor served as district judge, and was a member of the board of trustees and an unpaid professor of law at Baylor from 1845 until he died at Gay Hill in December, 1873.

110

110) The nuns at the Monastery of St. Clare raise and sell miniature horses. The monastery on SH 105 northeast of Brenham is open to visitors. The sisters of St. Clare moved here from Corpus Christi in 1985.

111

111) Dr. John Lockhart built this plantation house in Chappell Hill in 1850. It is one of the places Sam Houston is reputed to have stayed overnight. It was on what was then the main road between Houston and Austin; a road Houston often traveled.

112

112) The Richard Ganchons have restored the plantation Colonel W. W. Browning built in 1857 and their son-in-law, David Hannah III, has built an elaborate miniature railroad on the grounds. The plantation is just south of Chappell Hill and open for tours by appointment.

113

113) This old gin in Burton closed in 1973 but most of the machinery is still in working condition. It is being preserved.

114

114) The first church built in America by members of the Czech Brethren Protestant demonination still stands at Wesley. The interior is decorated with designs painted by Pastor B. E. Laciak in the late 1880s.

The Methodists organized Soule University at Chappell Hill in 1855. This school absorbed the male department of the earlier Chappell Hill Male and Female Institute and was later merged into Southwestern University at Georgetown. Chappell Hill was not named for a chapel, but for early settler Robert Chappell. Gay Hill was named not for a hill but for early settlers Thomas Gay and W. C. Hill. Independence was originally settled by John P. Coles and it was first called Coles' Settlement. The name was changed in 1836 to celebrate the Texas Declaration of Independence. Burton was founded in 1868 and named for John Burton.

Washington County was cotton country until after the Civil War. Many German settlers moved in when the plantations were broken up into farms. Most of the agricultural income now comes from livestock and poultry.

There is some oil and gas in Washington County. The oil was discovered in 1915. The gas was discovered much earlier. William Seidel was digging what he intended to be a water well on his farm at Greenvine in 1879 when he hit gas at 106 feet. Seidel ran a pipe to his house. He probably was the first Texan to enjoy gas heat.

Museum — Chappell Hill

Chappell Hill Historical Museum. Sunday afternoons. Donations.

Waco and Central Texas

McLennan, Coryell, Hamilton, Mills, Brown, Comanche, Bosque, Hill, Limestone, Robertson, Falls, and Bell counties.

The actual center of Texas is in McCulloch County, more than 100 miles southwest of Waco. But Waco has long claimed to be the "Heart of Texas" and it is so perceived, generally.

This area played an important role in Indian affairs before the white man came. There was a Waco Indian village about where the city of Waco is now. A plain near the Brazos, a few miles southeast of the village was already an established Indian council ground before the first Anglo colonists held their first parley and signed their first treaty here with the Waco, Tonkawa, Karankawa, and Tawakoni tribes in 1824.

Texas was not the ancestral home of all the Indian tribes the first Anglo settlers found here. The Wacos were a branch of the Wichita tribe. They came to Texas in the 1700s. The Comanches were a branch of the Shoshoni tribe and they came to Texas about the same time. The Cherokees and some others came to Texas because Anglo settlers had crowded them out of the southeastern United States.

McLennan County

The Comanches and the Apaches and the Kiowas were nomads and hunters. They lived mostly west of the Brazos River. The Indians living east of the Brazos were less nomadic and more inclined toward farming. The Brazos was a natural dividing line. The tribes met at a council ground near the river occasionally to talk out their territorial disputes. The differences they had had before must have seemed minor after the Anglo colonists began to arrive. The area that is now McLennan County was part of the grant the Mexican government made in 1825 to Robert Leftwich, later known as the Robertson Colony. The Texas Rangers established a small outpost in 1837 near an Indian village on the Brazos. The village had been occupied by Indians of the Waco tribe in Spanish times. They were evicted and displaced by Cherokees about 1830. Generations of Indians had been attracted to the site, where the city of Waco now stands, by a prolific spring.

1, previous page) Baylor University was named for Robert Emmett Bledsoe Baylor. He was born in Kentucky and he was a Baptist minister and lawyer when he came to Texas in 1839. He helped organize the Texas Baptist Education Society, wrote the university charter, and lobbied it through the Texas Congress in 1845. He was a district judge by the time Baylor University started classes at Independence but he also served as a volunteer, unpaid professor of law at the school until he died in 1853.

2) The Waco Indians had a village where the city of Waco is today. There was a major Indian council ground nearby and the government of the Republic of Texas authorized a trading post at the council ground before white settlement began. Sam Houston was a stockholder in the Torrey Trading Company, founded by David, Tom, and John Torrey.

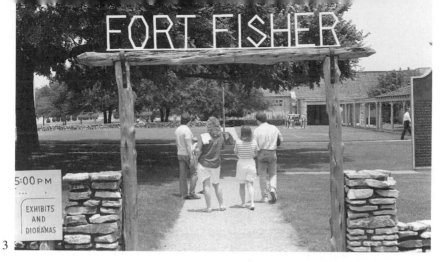

3) The Texas Rangers had a temporary camp near the Waco Indian Village as early as 1837. It was called Fort Fisher and the name survives in a city park near the original camp site.

Fort Fisher Park includes the Waco Visitors' Center, the headquarters of Texas Ranger Company F, a museum, and the Texas Ranger Hall of Fame. There is also an RV campground. Museum and Hall of Fame open every day except Thanksgiving, Christmas, and New Year's Day. Fee.

4) Waco has been the county seat since McLennan County was established. The present courthouse in Waco was built in 1902. The county was named for early settler Neil McLennan.

The presence of the Indian council grounds here prompted the Torrey Trading Houses to establish a branch in the area in 1843. Sam Houston was back in the president's office by this time. President Mirabeau Lamar had made war on the Indians during his two years as president. Houston resumed his previous policy of trying to manage the Indian problem with parleys and

71

5) One of the famous journalists of the 1890s lived and worked in Waco. William Cowper Brann had worked for several Texas newpapers before he started publishing The Iconoclast here in 1895. The Iconoclast was controversial and provocative. Brann often attacked Baylor and the Baptists and government agencies at all levels. He jokingly referred to Waco as the religious hub of the world. Brann was kidnapped and horsewhipped in 1897 and fatally wounded in 1898 in a sidewalk shootout provoked by a gambler named Tom Davis. Barnn always claimed his mission was to expose fakes and frauds. The word "Truth" is chiseled on his tombstone in Waco's Oakwood Cemetery, where former governors Sul Ross, Richard Coke, and Pat Neff also are buried.

6) The Armstrong-Browning Library on the Baylor campus houses the biggest collection of material related to Robert and Elizabeth Barrett Browning in the world. Dr. A. J. Armstrong was chairman of the English Department at Baylor from 1912 to 1952. He gave the school his personal collection of Browning writings in 1918 and the collection grew until it required a separate building. The present library building was dedicated in 1951. The collection includes a desk and chair used by Robert Browning as well as thousands of letters and manuscripts, and first editions of all of both poets' works.

The library is open to visitors weekdays 9 am to noon and 2 pm to 4 pm, Saturdays 9 am to noon. Donations encouraged.

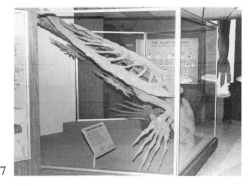

7

7) The Strecker Museum in the basement of the Sid Richardson Science Building on the Baylor campus claims to be the oldest continuously operating museum in Texas. This museum features an extensive collection of exhibits concerning natural history. It was named for John Kern Strecker, curator for 30 years until he died in 1933. Open weekdays 9 am to 4 pm, Saturdays 10 am to 1 pm, Sundays 2 pm to 5 pm. Free.

8

8) A collection of pioneer buildings and antiques Baylor alumnus Bill Daniel and his wife had assembled on their ranch in Liberty County has been reassembled on the Baylor campus, adjacent to the Brazos River. The Daniels donated the collection to the school to make sure it would be preserved. Bill Daniel was once governor of Guam, and the brother of former Texas governor Price Daniel.

treaties. The establishment of trading posts on the frontier was an official part of Houston's policy and Houston was a stockholder in the Torrey Trading Houses. Several meetings were held among the Indians and between the Indians and representatives of the republic on the grounds near the trading house between 1843 and 1845. Houston attended one of the meetings himself. The upshot was that Texas was technically at peace with all the tribes when Annexation was completed in 1845.

The first meeting between federal agents and the Texas tribes was held at the same council grounds in May of 1846. That meeting was peaceful and three thousand Indians held a peaceful pow-wow near the trading house in 1847. The goodwill later evaporated and all the agreements and treaties were broken and forgotten. But most of the later clashes between Indians and whites occurred farther north and west.

One of the early Anglo settlers in this area was Neil McLennan. He was born in Scotland and he lived in North Carolina and Florida before he and two of his brothers and their families moved to Texas in 1835. Both his brothers were killed by Indians before Neil McLennan built a home on the Bosque River near the present city of Waco in 1845. He lived here until he died in 1867. The legislature named this county for Neil McLennan when it

9

10

9) Waco preserves and cherishes the original Brazos River Bridge. This was the biggest suspension bridge in the country when it was finished in 1870. The ironwork was done by the firm that later built the Brooklyn Bridge. It is open now only to pedestrian traffic.

10) The Amicable Life Insurance Company Building in Waco was the tallest building west of the Mississippi in 1911. It is still the tallest building in Waco, at 22 floors.

was separated from Milam County in 1850. Waco has been the county seat from the beginning. The town site had been laid out only a year before the county was created.

One of the early residents of Waco was an Indian fighter with the improbable name of Shapley Prince Ross. He was one of the Robertson colonists from Kentucky. Ross joined the Texas Rangers in 1842 and he was stationed here in 1846. Ross put down roots. He started a ferry service on the Brazos. He built the first hotel in Waco and he was the first postmaster when the town got big enough to have a post office. Shapley Ross was the father of Texas Ranger Lawrence Sullivan "Sul" Ross, governor of Texas from 1887 to 1891 and later president of Texas A&M.

Baylor University has been in Waco since 1887. The school was started by the Baptists at Independence in 1845. Friction developed in the 1860s between Baylor President Rufus Burleson and the head of the Baylor Female Department. Another Baptist group offered Burleson a job as president of the Waco Classical School in Waco. Burleson accepted the offer and came here to head the school that was then renamed Waco University. The Baptist group sponsoring Baylor and the group sponsoring Waco University merged in 1886 to form the Baptist General Convention. The new organization combined the schools. The combined school was called Baylor and located in Waco. Rufus

11

11) *The Earle-Harrison house at 1901 North 5th in Waco was built in 1858 for Dr. and Mrs. Baylis Earle and later owned by General Thomas Harrison. The house was restored in 1969 and it is open to visitors by appointment. Fee.*

12

12) *The house known as East Terrace is maintained by the Historic Waco Foundation. It was built about 1872 for John W. Mann. 100 Mill Street. Open 2 pm to 5 pm, Saturday and Sunday. Fee.*

Burleson was named president of the combined school. The separate Baylor Female College was moved at the same time from Independence to Belton and the name was changed in 1934 to Mary Hardin Baylor.

Baylor University is the oldest institution of higher learning in Texas still operating under the original name. The campus is on the near southeast side of Waco just off I-35.

One of the worst tornadoes in Texas history hit Waco in May of 1953. That storm killed 114 people, and destroyed 150 homes and 196 business buildings.

Bellmead is the second biggest town in McLennan County. It was established in 1924 and named for a farm in Tennessee. The original business in Bellmead was a shop devoted to rebuilding locomotives for the Missouri, Kansas, and Texas Railroad. McGregor was established in 1882 when the Cotton Belt Railroad came through. It was named for landowner G. C.

13

13) *Wholesale grocer M. A. Cooper built this elaborate house at 1801 Austin Street in Waco in 1906. His son, Madison Cooper, inherited the house and in an attic room here in the 1950s he wrote the surprise best-selling novel* Sironia, Texas. *Madison Cooper died in 1956 and left his fortune in a foundation to benefit Waco. The Cooper Foundation and Historic Waco Foundation jointly restored the Cooper home in 1986. It houses the Cooper Foundation and it is open to the public on a limited basis.*

14

14) *The city of Waco built its first water pumping station in 1904 on what is now Mill Street. The building was expanded and then used for several other purposes after the city built newer pumping stations. The original pumping station building now houses an eatery called the Waterworks Restaurant.*

15

15) *Lumber merchant William Cameron built this house overlooking the junction of the Bosque and Brazos rivers as a summer home. The Cameron house at 1300 College Drive now houses the Waco Art Center. Open Tuesday through Saturday, 10 am to 5 pm, Sunday, 1 pm to 5 pm.*

76

16) *Prescriptions and fountain drinks are still being dispensed in a building in Moody that has been a drug store since 1882. The ownership has changed and some of the old fixtures are gone, but the building is almost as old as the town. Moody was established in 1881 when the Gulf, Colorado, and Santa Fe Railroad came through. It was named for W. L. Moody of Galveston, one of the railroad directors.*

16

17

17) *The railroads once had more imaginative people promoting rail travel. W. G. Crush was one of the most imaginative. He persuaded 30,000 people to buy tickets on Katy excursion trains to see a locomotive collision he staged near West in 1896. Crush built a tent city and sold advertising on the freight cars coupled to the doomed locomotives. The crash was spectacular. But flying debris killed two spectators and injured a dozen others. Scott Joplin composed a song about the Crash at Crush and the Katy railroad paid several damage claims.*

McGregor. The settlement of Willow Springs was established in 1876. It was renamed Mart when the International and Great Northern Railroad came through in 1901 because the residents thought the railroad would make their town a big trade center. Moody was established in 1881 when the Gulf, Colorado, and Santa Fe Railroad came through. It was named for railroad director W. L. Moody of Galveston.

This was the heart of the cotton belt before cotton farming moved west. There is still some cotton grown in McLennan County but most of the agricultural income now comes from livestock and poultry. The county has some modest deposits of oil and gas.

Museums — Waco

Earle-Napier House (1868), 814 S. 4th.
Fort House (1868), 503 S. 4th.
McCulloch House (1866), 407 Columbus.
(Houses maintained by Historic Waco Foundation, open Saturday and Sunday
    afternoons. Fee.)

Coryell County

Indians of several tribes occupied this area without serious interference in Spanish times. The Mexican government granted it in 1825 to Robert Leftwich and it became part of the Robertson Colony. A Robertson colonist named James Coryell obtained a grant in 1835 where Coryell Creek joins the Leon River. It is not clear whether Coryell ever lived on his land. Texas was in turmoil in 1835. There was a dispute between the Austin and Robertson colonies. Coryell apparently spent most of his time and energy helping protect the Robertson claims. He was a member of Sterling Robertson's ranger com-

18

18) The outpost the U.S. Army built in 1849 near what was to become the city of Gatesville was one of the first units in the chain of forts developed to protect the frontier. There were 17 buildings here and the 18th was under construction when the army decided to abandon the post, in 1852. Nothing is left of Fort Gates. The site is now a horse farm.

19) The first public building built in Gatesville was a jail and it survives. It was built about 1858 and it stands now in Raby Park in Gatesville.

19

20) Gatesville has been the county seat since Coryell County was created in 1854. The present courthouse was built in 1872.

20

pany in 1835 and 1836. He was with T. H. Barron's company of rangers in 1837 when he was killed by Indians.

There was no serious attempt to settle this area until after Texas joined the United States. The U.S. Army built a chain of forts, then, to protect settlers and travelers. One of the early forts was here on the Leon River. The army built it in 1849 and named it Fort Gates for Major C. R. Gates. He was one of the heroes of the Mexican War. The settlement that grew up nearby took the name of Major Gates, too, and became Gatesville.

The Texas Consultation of 1835 gave the Robertson Colony the designation Municipality of Milam. The municipality became Milam County in 1836. This area was included in Bell County when it was separated from the original Milam County in 1850. This county was separated from Bell County in 1854 and named for James Coryell.

21) *Pat Neff was born in western McLennan County in 1871. He was elected governor in 1920. His mother died the same year Neff took office. She bequeathed six acres of land she owned in eastern Coryell County to the public. Governor Neff two years later proposed the creation of a state Parks Board. He said his mother's bequest gave him the idea.*

21

22) *Just about all there is of the business district of The Grove in eastern Coryell County belongs to an antiques dealer from Austin. Moody Anderson wanted to buy the teller cage from the former Planters' State Bank. The owner refused to sell unless Anderson took the whole building, so Anderson bought it, and got the former bank, the former post ofice, and the old general store. The building is filled with antiques and old-time mrchandise and open to visitors . on weekends.*

22

The army had abandoned Fort Gates by 1854 because the frontier had moved farther west. But the town of Gatesville survived to become the county seat. Gatesville is still the county seat but Copperas Cove has become a bigger town because of another army fort.

The U.S. Army bought 160,000 acres of land in southwest Coryell County in 1942 and turned it into a training base. Camp Hood was devoted in the beginning to training crews for tank destroyers. Activity at the base subsided for a while after the end of World War II. But the Second Armored Division was assigned to the base in 1946. The name was changed from Camp Hood to Fort Hood and the base became one of the most important in the country. The Second Armored and the First Cavalry Divisions both are based here.

Gatesville was best known for many years as the home of the Gatesville School for Boys. The buildings are still here, but they are now part of the Texas Department of Corrections. The T.D.C. keeps women prisoners here. The Texas Youth Council now keeps young offenders in schools at Brownwood, Giddings, Gainesville, Pyote, and Crockett.

Coryell County is part of the limestone hill country. There is some farming but sheep, goats, cattle, and horses produce most of the agricultural income.

Museum — Gatesville

Coryell County Museum. 8th and Sanders. Weekends. Free.

Park — The Grove

Mother Neff State Park. Hiking, camping. Fee.

Hamilton County

The area that now constitutes Hamilton County was divided in colonial days between the Robertson Colony and the second Stephen F. Austin Colony. But the area was left to the Indians until after Texas separated from Mexico and joined the United States. The Robertson Colony became Milam County and the second Austin Colony became Bastrop County after the Texas Revolution succeeded in 1836 and these original counties were subsequently split

23

23) The government of Hamilton County carries on its business in a courthouse built of local limestone in 1887. There is a small historical museum in the courthouse, open to the public during normal business hours: weekdays, 8 am to 5 pm.

24) This is the edge of the Hill Country. Building stone is plentiful and many of the early stone houses are in sound condition. This is the Francis Graves home at 201 West Ross.

24

up into smaller counties. The congress of the republic took land from Bosque, Comanche, and Lampasas counties to create this county in 1842. Bosque and Comanche had originally been part of Milam County. Lampasas County had originally been part of Bastrop County and Milam County.

Texas once had a governor named Hamilton but he never had a county named for him. This county was named for a former governor of South Carolina. Texans were indebted to James Hamilton for several things. He donated money to the Texas Army during the revolution. In 1839 he was commissioned by President Mirabeau Lamar to try to negotiate a loan for the Republic of Texas. Hamilton did negotiate several treaties between Texas and foreign powers in pursuing that objective. But he never found anyone willing to lend $5 million to the fledgling republic. He might have accomplished it eventually but Sam Houston abandoned the loan scheme and dismissed Hamilton when he returned to the president's office in 1841.

James Hamilton estimated that the government of Texas owed him $200,000 for the work he had done and the expenses he had incurred trying to arrange the loan. He was on his way to Texas to try to collect when the ship he was traveling on was wrecked in the Gulf of Mexico, in 1857. Hamilton drowned.

This county never had been organized after it was created in 1842. The legislature recreated it in 1858. A county government was organized and the county seat was placed at a settlement in the valley of Pecan Creek, also named for James Hamilton.

The first Anglo settlers here were members of the Robert Carter family. They came in 1854. There were fewer than 500 people in the county when the Civil War began, and some of them left during the war because the area was so exposed to Indian attacks. Comanche raids continued here until after

25

the end of the Civil War. The Indians killed a school teacher here in 1866, and a Baptist preacher in 1867. This was a hotbed of secession sentiment in the years preceding the Civil War. The vote on secession in Hamilton County was 86 in favor and 1 against.

The population of Hamilton County reached 13,500 in 1900 and remained at about that level until World War II. The population has been declining since that time and is now less than 9,000. About one third of the population of the county lives in Hamilton, the county seat.

Hico is the second biggest town. Hico was founded in 1856 by J. R. Alford and named for some local Indians. The settlement was originally situated about two miles south of the present site. Hico moved in 1880 to get on the rail line when the Houston and Texas Central came through the county.

Carlton, in the north end of the county, was settled in the 1870s by a family named Charlton and the town was called Charlton until the post office was established. The spelling was changed then to Carlton. Fairy was named for Fairy Fort. She was the daughter of one of the original settlers. Pottsville was named for settler John Potts. Aleman is said to have been named for an early Spanish settlement. Shive was settled in the 1870s and named for early settlers J. W. and R. L. Shive.

Farming was the principal occupation here until World War II. There is far more ranching than farming now, and some oil and gas.

Mills County

The Apaches and Comanches were still contesting for control of this area when the first Spanish explorers came through in 1786. The Spanish attempted no settlements or missions here. The Comanches won the contest with the Apaches and resisted the intrusion of the Anglos. They were killing settlers up until 1868.

Most of what is now Mills County was included in the Robertson Colony in colonial days. Jesse Hanna and John Williams were among the first settlers. Hanna and his five sons established a settlement they called Hanna Valley on the Colorado River in 1856. John Williams started ranching in 1855 near the present town of Mullin. A settlement grew up at the Williams Ranch. There was a school and a trading post. A grist mill established in 1878 helped make the Williams Ranch Settlement the principal trading center in the area.

26   27

26) Mills County built a stone jail the same year the county government was created, in 1887. This building served as the county jail until 1977.

27) The community of Mullin was founded by Charles Mullin in 1857. The Mullin United Methodist Church was built in 1896 and rebuilt in 1920.

There was a hotel by 1884 and several saloons. The population reached a peak of about 250. The first railroad came to the area in 1885 and changed everything.

The Gulf, Colorado, and Santa Fe laid tracks well to the south of the Williams Ranch Settlement. The railroad created some new towns. One of them was named for railroad official Joseph Goldthwaite. This new town became the trade center. Most of the people at the Williams Ranch settlement moved to Goldthwaite. The people moving into the area because of the new railroad soon began to feel that they should have their own county. The legislature obliged them in 1887 by detaching some land from Brown, Lampasas, Comanche, and Hamilton counties to create a new county with Goldthwaite as the county seat. The county was named for John T. Mills. He was a native of Ireland. He got a law degree in Tennessee before he came to Texas in 1837. Mills was a district judge during the period of the republic. He was a candidate for governor in 1849 but he finished third in a three-man field. Mills died in Marshall in 1871, probably without ever seeing the area that would become Mills County.

The population of Mills County reached a peak of almost 10,000 in 1910, when there was much more farming. The population is now only about half the 1910 total. Goldthwaite is the biggest town but its population is under 2,000. Mullin was established on the Gulf, Colorado, and Santa Fe rail line in 1888. Priddy was established about 1885 and named for landowner Thomas Priddy. Caradan was established in 1899 and named for landowners Smith Caraway and Dan Bush.

There was a substantial amount of cotton farming in Mills County in earlier times. Most of the farm income now comes from livestock. No significant mineral deposits have been discovered in Mills County.

Museum — Goldthwaite

Mills County Historical Museum. 3rd and Fisher. Monday, Wednesday, Friday, and Saturday afternoons. Free.

28) *Williams Ranch Settlement near Mullin was the principal town in Mills County before the railroad came. Only the cemetery remains at Williams Ranch Settlement. Founder John Williams is buried here.*

28

29) *Mills County has one of the few surviving highway suspension bridges in Texas. The Regency suspension bridge is listed in the* National Register of Historic Places. *Two earlier bridges built at this location failed. This one outlasted the need. The communities it served, Regency and Hanna Valley, have disappeared. The bridge is a ghost of the past, on a dirt road off FM 574.*

29

Brown County _____

Neither the Spanish nor the Mexicans seriously interfered with the Indians in this part of Texas and the Comanches still considered it their territory when the first Anglo settlers began to move in during the early 1850s. The legislature took part of Comanche County and part of Travis County in 1856 to create this county. The county government was organized in 1858 and the county was named for Henry S. Brown. He was born in Kentucky and came to Texas in 1824. Brown fought in several campaigns against the Indians betwen 1825 and 1832. He died in 1834. Brownwood has been the county seat from the beginning. It also was named for Henry Brown.

Indian attacks discouraged settlement until the 1870s. There were only 200 people in the county in 1858 when the county government was organized. There were fewer than 600 settlers in the county in 1879 and the whole area was still open range. There were some clashes between the pioneer ranchers and the farmers when farmers began to move into the area in 1880.

Brown County is one of the state's major pecan producers. Pecans were growing wild in Texas long before the first Anglo settlers came. Native pecans were being exported from Texas by the 1850s. An Englishman named F. A.

30) *A new Brown County Jail was built in 1981. The old jail built in 1902 is now the county museum of history with exhibits concerning pioneer days and the evolution of communications. 200 block of North Broadway. Saturdays, March to November, 9 am to 3 pm.*

30

31) *The house wholesale grocer J. A. Walker built at 701 Center Street in Brownwood in 1901 has survived to gain a listing in the* National Register of Historic Places. *It is a private residence and not open to the public.*

31

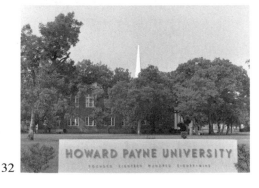

32) *Howard Payne University in Brownwood was established by Rev. J. D. Robnett and the Pecan Valley Baptist Association in 1889 as Howard Payne College. It became a university in 1973. Howard Payne was Robnett's brother-in-law and a major contributor to the school.*

32

Swinden did some of the early work toward improving the native pecan at an orchard he established in 1884 in Brown County.

The settlement that became Brownwood was originally located on the east bank of Pecan Bayou. The population moved to the west bank after Greenleaf

Fish donated land for a new townsite there. Fish came to Texas from New York. He fought at the Battle of San Jacinto and received his land here in payment for that service. Fish settled on his property in Brown County in 1860 and died here in 1888.

Brookesmith in southwestern Brown County was named for railroad promoter Brookes Smith. It is on the site of an 1863 Texas Ranger camp. Bangs was established in the west central part of the county in the 1880s and named for Samuel Bangs because he once owned the land. Bangs was a pioneer Texas printer. Blanket is said to have been so named because the first setttlers found an Indian blanket at the site. Cross Cut was originally named Cross Out. The Post Office Department evidently changed the spelling by mistake. May was named for early settler W. D. May. More than half the population of the county lives in Brownwood.

Martin Meichinger of Brownwood discovered oil on his property in 1884 while he was drilling for water. But serious exploration for oil did not begin until 1917. Several fields were discovered and there was an oil boom between 1920 and 1927 in Brown County.

There was a bigger boom when the U.S. Army built Camp Bowie outside Brownwood to train troops for World War II. The 36th Division was one of

33

33) The Douglas MacArthur Academy of Freedom features displays dealing with the evolution of personal freedom and some of the late general's souvenirs. The academy at Coggin and Austin in Brownwood is open for tours daily during the school year. It is affiliated with Howard Payne University.

34

34) The U.S. Army has had two training camps in Texas named for Texas hero Jim Bowie. The original Camp Bowie was built during World War I, outside of Fort Worth. That camp closed after World War I ended. The Army built a new Camp Bowie outside Brownwood in 1940. This one originally was a training base for the 36th Division of the Texas National Guard, but many other units trained here before the base was closed at the end of World War II. The area is now an industrial park but there is a collection of military hardware in the 36th Division Memorial Park at Burnett Drive and Travis Road.

the units trained at Camp Bowie. The base opened in December of 1940 and closed in August of 1946. It has since been turned into an industrial park.

The principal enterprise in Brown County in the early days was ranching and most of the agricultural income today comes from livestock. But crops of peanuts, wheat,and feed grains are grown and farms irrigated by water from Lake Brownwood produce vegetables. Brown County Water Improvement District No. 1 created Lake Brownwood in 1931 by building a dam on Pecan Bayou.

Park — Brownwood

Lake Brownwood State Park, off SH 279. Camping. Fee.

Comanche County

This county is part of the vast area once called the Comanchia, where the Comanche Indians held sway for 150 years until the middle 1870s. The Comanchia extended from Kansas to northern Mexico. It included most of West Texas and part of New Mexico. The Comaches never settled the area. They were nomads, not given to settling. They discovered the horses the Spanish had brought to the New World and in the early 1700s the Comanches became expert horsemen and horse thieves. Some historians say there were never more than 10,000 or 12,000 Comanches in Texas. But they ranged so

35

35) The little log cabin that served as the Comanche County Courthouse when the county seat was at Cora in the 1850s now occupies a corner of the courthouse square in Comanche. The old Cora courthouse went into private hands when the county government moved to Comanche in 1859. It was moved several times and it was a private museum for a time before the county reclaimed it in 1983 and moved it here.

36

36) *The old Comanche National Bank Building became a dress shop when the bank built a new building nearby. The old building and the new one, too, are on the courthouse square in Comanche.*

far and punished intruders with such ferocity that they delayed settlement of West Texas for many years.

The Comanches split off from the Shoshoni tribe on the northern Great Plains about 1700 and moved southward to hunt buffalo. The Comanches had even less patience with white men's ways than other Indians had. They were hunters. They never developed any interest in any other way of life. Some historians say the word Comanche is a Spanish version of the Ute Indian word for enemy. The Comanches' relations with other Indians were not much better than their relations with the whites. Some of the early Spanish missions were established to protect the Apaches from the Comanches. Most white settlers, and the Mexicans and the Spanish before them, regarded the Comanches as a scourge. The Comanches referred to themselves as "The People" or "The Real Human Beings."

The area that is now Comanche County was part of the original Milam County. The first Anglo settlers arrived in 1852. There were only a few dozen families here when the legislature created the county in 1856 and named it for the Comanche Indians. A little settlement known originally as Troy was the first county seat. The residents changed the name of the settlement to Cora when it became the seat of the county government. Cora was the name of one of the daughters of early settler Alonzo Beeman. Cora was the county seat until 1859 when the government moved to Comanche to be closer to the center of the county. Comanche was established in 1878 when John Duncan donated the town site.

The U.S. Army road from Fort Gates in Coryell County to Fort Phantom Hill near the present city of Abilene passed through Comanche County. This was called the Corn Road because so many of the wagon trains using it were hauling feed for the army's horses. The traffic on the Corn Road discouraged Indian raiders until 1861. The U.S. troops left then for the Civil War and the Texas Frontier Regiments never had enough manpower to deter the Comanches.

37) The Comanche County Historical Museum at Moorman and Hillcrest on the west side of Comanche is open Sunday afternoons and by appointment. Free.

The Indians stole the settlers' horses during the war and scattered their cattle. They killed and kidnapped settlers until many of the pioneer familiies gave up and moved farther east. The population dropped to about 60 at one point during the Civil War. Conditions improved after the war ended but the Indian attacks didn't end until about 1870. The newspaper *Comanche Chief* started publishing in Comanche in 1873, and the newspaper exclaimed in one of its early editions that nobody had been killed by Indians in Comanche County in three or four years.

The first railroad to reach this county was the Houston and Texas Central. The railroad established the town of DeLeon. Comanche did not get rail service until 1891 when the Fort Worth and Denver arrived.

Oil was discovered at Sipe Springs in 1918 and there was a brief boom, but the county is not now a major oil producer. Ranching was the chief enterprise here from the beginning. Some of the landholders shifted to farming around 1900. Cotton was the main crop until the boll weevil got here about 1914. Peanuts are the chief crop now and the county has about 30,000 acres under irrigation. But most of the agricultural income still comes from livestock.

Parks — Lake Proctor

U.S. Corps of Engineers maintains 4 parks around the lake east of Comanche. Accessible from US 377 or SH 16.

Bosque County_____

Fernando del Bosque led one of the early Spanish expeditions into Texas in 1675 but he probably never got this far north and it was not for Fernando that this county and the river were named. Bosque is the Spanish word for woody or wooded place. This probably is the reason the Marquis de Aguayo applied the name to the river in 1719. The north and east branches of the Bosque River meet and join here. Bosque County was named for the river.

38

38) *Texas Safari outside Clifton is one of the premier drive-through wildlife parks in Texas. A. C. Parsons started the ranch here as a private retreat for his family. He collected so many exotic animals that people suggested he should open it to the public and he did. Texas Safari Ranch opened in May of 1981 and it has been growing ever since. The entrance is off SH 6 just west of Clifton. Fee.*

39   40

39) *Bosque County has a Norwegian flavor and Cleng Peerson was responsible for it. Peerson was a native of Norway. He was not a Quaker but he got interested in trying to find homes in the New World for some Quakers who were not very welcome in Norway. Peerson arranged for the immigration of many Norwegians to the states around the Great Lakes and then decided to settle in Texas in 1850. A number of Norwegian families did likewise and many of their descendants still live around Clifton and Cranfills Gap.*

40) *One of the Norwegian immigrants here developed a plow that is said to have been the forerunner of the disc plow. It is one of the exhibits in the Bosque Memorial Museum, in Clifton. 10 am to 5 pm, Friday and Saturday, and 2 pm to 5 pm Sunday. Fee.*

91

41

41) *Dozens of historic buildings and ruins in southwestern Bosque County are listed in the* National Register of Historic Places. *Norway Mill on FM 182 southwest of Clifton was built in 1870. The machinery was steam powered. The mill closed in 1890.*

42

42) *St. Olaf's Lutheran Church outside Cranfills Gap was built of local stone by the Norwegians in 1886. It is said that the Norwegians were attracted to this part of Texas because the landscape is similar to that in eastern Norway.*

This county was part of the old Robertson Colony but there was no settlement here in colonial days. The area was part of McLennan County when the first settlers arrived. The English Universal Immigration Company bought 27,000 acres of land here in 1850 and brought 30 families over from England to establish a community they called Kent. Some of those families decided when they got here to make their own arrangements for land in less lonesome places. The others abandoned the colony about 1852 and Kent disappeared.

Norwegian immigrants began settling in the western part of Bosque County in 1854. That was the year the legislature separated this area from McLennan County and created a new county. The town of Meridian was laid out by pioneer surveyor George Erath on the 4th of July, 1854. It has been the county seat ever since. Some Germans settled in the eastern part of the county after the Civil War but most of the settlers here came from the southeastern United

43) The Meridian State Recreation Area has a small lake and provisions for picnicking and camping. There are also screened shelters for rent. This park is one of those developed by the Civilian Conservation Corps in the 1930s. It is off SH 22, four miles southwest of Meridian.

States. The settlers had some skirmishes with the Indians but there were no Indian raids recorded here after 1868.

The old Chisholm cattle trail came through Bosque County and many of the early cowboy ballads might have been lost if the trail had followed some other course. The Chisholm Trail passed close by the home of settlers James and Susan Lomax. Their son, John Avery Lomax got very interested in the songs he heard the cowboys singing as they rode the trail or sat around their campfires. Lomax began to write down what he heard while he was a boy here and he continued for the rest of his life to collect and record and publish old ballads and folk songs and spirituals. He became one of the founders of the Texas Folklore Society in 1909.

The first railroad to reach Bosque was the Texas Central in 1880. It stopped at Walnut Springs and created a little boom. The Santa Fe reached Meridian in 1881. Meridian is the second biggest city in the county. Clifton has about twice the population of Meridian but the total population of the county is only about 15,000. Clifton moved to its present location in 1881 to get on the railroad. It was established in 1854 on a cliff on the bank of the Bosque, hence the name.

Valley Mills was established in 1854 and named for an early grist mill. Morgan was named for Thomas Morgan. Cranfills Gap was named for early settler George Cranfill. Ward Keeler named Iredell for his son Ire.

Farmers in Bosque County grow some cotton, peanuts, and grains. But livestock and poultry produce most of the agricultural income here. There is a little oil.

Hill County _____

The Comanches controlled this part of Texas while it was part of Mexico. Neither the Mexicans nor the Spanish before them made any attempt at settlement here but they didn't want anybody else settling, either. The American adventurer Philip Nolan traveled extensively around Texas between 1791 and 1801. Nolan represented himself as a horse trader looking for animals to take to Louisiana, but the Spanish always considered him an intruder and spy. The Spanish governor issued orders in 1800 that Nolan was to be arrested if he entered Texas again. Spanish troops killed him in 1801 when he resisted their attempts to arrest him. It is not certain where this happened, but it may have been near the present town of Blum in what is now northwest Hill County.

There were no attempts at Anglo settlement here until after Texas separated from Mexico and became a state. A band of Taovaya Indians had a village on the Brazos near the present town of Whitney. The Taovayas were a branch of the Wichita tribe and the Comanches tolerated them because the Taovayas did some farming and raised food the Comanches never had the patience to grow but did like to eat. They were trading partners. The Taovayas made the first Anglos feel unwelcome. Anglos didn't come in any numbers until after the Texas Rangers established Fort Smith near the present town of Itasca in 1846 and the U.S. Army established Fort Graham near the present town of Whitney in 1848. Fort Smith was named for Ranger Thomas I. Smith and Fort Graham was named for one of the heroes of the Mexican War. Both forts were abandoned and closed in 1850 after settlers moved in and the frontier moved farther west.

This area was included in the original Robertson County in 1837. Part of Robertson County became Navarro County in 1846 and the legislature took part of Navarro County in 1853 to create this county. It was named for George Washington Hill. He came to Texas from Tennessee in 1836. Hill served

44) The powerful people in Texas during the revolution and the days of the Republic might have been called the Tennessee Mafia if the expression had been in use then. Great numbers of them came from Tennessee, as did George Washington Hill. He was an Indian agent, member of the Texas congress and Secretary of War. It was for him that this county was named.

44

45

46

45) The Hill County Courthouse in Hillsboro is one of the more distinguished 19th century courthouses still in use in Texas. It was designed by W. C. Dodson and built in 1889.

46) This monument in the little family cemetery on FM 66 east of Itasca marks the grave of pioneer David S. Files. The area where he settled in 1846 is still called Files Valley. The Files family donated the land for the nearby Southwestern Presbyterian Home for Orphans.

briefly in the Texas Army and then in the congress of the republic. He was Indian Agent for the republic and secretary of war during Sam Houston's second term as president of the republic.

The citizens of the new county chose the location for the county seat in an election, and the town built on the site they chose was named Hillsboro for the same George Washington Hill. The first courthouse was built of logs in 1854. The post office was established in Hillsboro in 1856. The first railroad came to Hill County in 1879. The Texas Central created the towns of Whitney and Aquilla. Whitney was named for a Texas Central stockholder. Aquilla was named for Aquilla Creek.

The St. Louis and Southwestern built a line into Hill County in 1881 and created the town of Hubbard. There had been a small settlement at the site earlier but it had no formal name. It had been called Slap Out, McLainsboro, and Liberty Hill at different times. The railroad promoted a sale of town lots. Former Governor Richard Hubbard attended the sale. Somebody suggested the town should be named for him, and it was.

The railroad brought a short period of good times to Hubbard because the town had a well producing hot mineral water. Many people were convinced in those days that drinking and bathing in hot mineral water improved their health. Several towns with such wells and rail service became health resorts and flourished. But the health boom in Hubbard played out when the hot well caved in and could not be induced to produce any more mineral water. A

47) Cotton was once the mainstay of the economy here. The economy is more diversified now, and Hill County farms produce more feed grains than cotton.

48) Lake Whitney State Recreation Area on FM 1244 just southwest of Whitney has campsites and hookups and shelters for rent. There is also an airstrip. Fee. The Army Corps of Engineers also maintains 19 parks around Lake Whitney, part of the Brazos River flood control program.

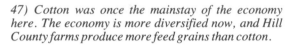

49) The baseball legend Tristram Speaker was born in Hill County in 1888. He started playing ball for Cleburne in 1906. He also played for Houston before he reached the majors where he became the greatest centerfielder of his time. Tris Speaker was buried in Hubbard when he died in 1958. This likeness is from the plaque in the National Baseball Hall of Fame in Cooperstown, New York.

49

50) Hubbard has a number of comfortable homes left from the boom days. This is the McDaniel house at Third and Maple.

50

tornado destroyed some of Hubbard's treaured buildings in 1973 but several fine homes from the boom days survive.

Itasca got on the map when the Missouri, Kansas, and Texas Railroad came through in 1881. It supposedly was named for Lake Itasca in Minnesota.

The early railroads created some towns and killed some others. An energetic family named Gathings from Mississippi started a settlement in northern Hill County in the 1850s. It was named Covington, for the family of James Gathings' wife. The Gathings started a school and a mill and a shoe factory. But the early railroads missed Covington and people moved to the railroad towns, leaving Covington to become a ghost of what it was.

Hill County was plantation country before the Civil War and cotton continued to be the major crop here for a long time after the plantations were broken up into farms. The county's economy is more diversified now with substantial ranching and manufacturing but farmers here still grow cotton, peanuts, and grains. Oil production is not significant.

Museum — Hillsboro

Confederate Research Center and Gun Museum, Hill College. 8 am to 5 pm, weekdays during school terms.

Limestone County

The Tawakoni Indians were living in this part of Texas when the first Spanish explorer came through in 1720. The Tawakonis had been crowded

51

51) The log village and stockade built by the James and Silas Parker families in what is now Limestone County in 1834 have been rebuilt twice. Nothing is left of the original structures. The present replica was designed by architect Raiford Stripling and built with cedar logs from Buescher State Park at Smithville. The fort is maintained by the Texas Parks and Wildlife Department as a state historic site. Fee.

52) *Cynthia Ann Parker married a Comanche chief and bore him several children after she was kidnapped from the family stockade at the age of nine. The Indians also killed several members of the Parker family in that raid on Fort Parker in 1836.*

52

out of Kansas by the Comanches and by 1800 the Comanches were crowding them here too.

The first Anglo settlers in what is now Limestone County came in 1834. They were the James and Silas Parker families. Five other families settled with the Parkers at what they called Fort Parker. The fort was a little cluster of cabins protected by a log stockade and surrounded by fields where the settlers grew their food. Several hundred Comanche and Kiowa warriors attacked the little settlement one day in May of 1836. The Indians killed five of the settlers and wounded two others. They kidnapped Silas Parker's children and three other survivors.

The Comanches raised young Cynthia Ann and John Parker as Indians. Cynthia was nine when she was kidnapped and John was six. Cynthia eventually married Comanche chief Peta Nocona and they had several children before Texas Rangers recaptured Cynthia in 1860. Cynthia thought of herself as a Comanche and she never readjusted to white ways. She and the baby daughter she was nursing when she was recaptured both died in 1864.

The Parker family made several attempts to rescue John Parker. He was not located until he was grown and he made it plain then that he wanted to stay with the Indians. He married a Mexican woman. John served briefly in the Confederate Army during the Civil War but he returned to his wife in Mexico at the end of the war.

One of the sons Cynthia Ann had with Peta Nocona became the war chief of his tribe. Quanah Parker led the Comanches in their last hopeless defense of their hunting grounds in West Texas. He and a few other survivors finally gave up and went to live on the Indian Reservation in Oklahoma in 1875. Quanah visited his mother's family in Texas after that and he visited John Parker in Mexico. Quanah's descendants and the descendants of the Texas Parkers hold joint reunions at the Fort Parker State Park near the Navasota River outside Groesbeck.

The survivors of the massacre at Fort Parker moved after the attack and settled in what is now Anderson County. Limestone County pioneer Hampton Steele wrote in his brief history of Limestone County that there was no further attempt to settle here until Logan Stroud came in 1842.

The Steeles and a few other families were here by 1844. Hampton Steele said they often had nothing to eat except the game they killed and his father had to haul his corn 50 miles to get it milled.

The legislature separated this area from the original Robertson County in 1846 to create a new county. It was named for the limestone that lies under much of the area. The only town of any consequence at the time was Springfield. Settlement actually started at Springfield in 1838 but the first settlers were frightened away by the Indians after a few months. The settlers returned in 1844 and Springfield was designated the county seat when the county was organized. The town took its name from a large spring at the site.

The people of Springfield were unlucky or uncommonly careless. Two courthouses were destroyed by fire and all the county records were lost before the residents of the county decided in 1874 to move the government to Groesbeck. The move had less to do with fires than with transportation. The Houston and Texas Central missed Springfield when it extended its rail line into Limestone County in 1869. New towns developed on the rail line. Kosse was named for railroad surveyor Theodore Kosse. Groesbeck was named for railroad director Abram Groesbeeck, with a little modification in the spelling.

53

53) This ruin stands on the highest ground in one of the oldest towns in Limestone County. Tehuacana was settled in the 1840s on land the Mexican government granted to John Boyd in 1835. The Presbyterians started Trinity University in this building in 1868. Trinity University moved to Waxahachie in 1902 and then to San Antonio in 1942. The Presbyterians gave this building to the Methodists. They moved their Westminister College here from Collin County and it was here until it was merged into Southwestern University in 1950. The Westminister alumni organization has been trying to buy the building.

54) Confederate veterans of the Civil War established a reunion campground in Limestone County in 1892. The Confederate Reunion Campground is now a state park, with no provisions for camping.

55) The oldest house in Mexia was built before the town was established. The Henry-Martin-Dorsett house was built in 1852. The site on SH 14 south of Mexia was a plantation then. It is a subdivision now, with several oil wells. Mexia is pronounced "muh-HAY-uh".

56) The Historical Museum of Limestone County in an old commercial building in Groesbeck is devoted mostly to local history. 210 West Navasota Street. Open Tuesday through Saturday, 2 pm to 4 pm. Fee.

56

Groesbeck is still the county seat but Mexia is about twice its size. Mexia was also established when the Houston and Texas Central came through. It was named for landowner Jorge Mexia. Coolidge, in the north end of the county, was originally called Armour. The name was changed in 1903 to honor one of the stockholders of the Trinity and Brazos Valley Railroad when it came through. Thornton was established in the 1850s and named for early settler John Thornton. Tehuacana was founded in the 1840s and named for the Tawakoni Indians.

German prisoners of war were housed in a camp at Mexia during World War II. The Mexia State School for the Retarded was established on the old P.O.W. camp site in 1946.

Gas was discovered near Mexia in 1912. There was a little oil production before 1920 but the big oil discovery here came in 1921. Two gushers came in on the same August day that year and the population of Mexia jumped from 4,000 to 40,000 in a few days. The oil production has declined substantially since the early days but there are lignite deposits in Limestone County, too. The Brazos River Authority completed a dam and reservoir on the

Navasota River in 1979 to supply cooling water for power plants fueled by lignite from Limestone and Robertson counties.

Lumbering and plantation farming were the chief enterprises here in the early days. Farmers now raise some cotton, feed grains, and peaches, but there is far more ranching than farming. The oil earns more money than the farming and ranching combined.

Park — Mexia

Fort Parker State Park, off SH 14, southwest of Mexia. Camping. Fee.

57

57) Many relics of the oil boom of the 1920s still stand around the western outskirts of Mexia. The boom reached its peak in 1922. It drew thousands of new people to Mexia. Governor Pat Neff at one stage declared martial law and sent the Texas Rangers and the National Guard to Mexia to stop the oilfield workers from drinking and gambling and killing each other.

Robertson County

Elements of the Tawakoni, Kichai, Waco, Caddo, Anadarko, Delaware, and Cherokee Indians were living in what is now Robertson County before the first settlers came. Domingo Teran probably came through here in 1690 and it is likely that Domingo Ramon was here in 1716, but neither stayed and there were no settlements until after 1825, when the Mexican government authorized the Texas Association of Tennessee to bring in some Anglos from the United States.

The Texas Association was organized in Nashville, Tennessee in 1822 by Mayor Felix Robertson and his cousin Sterling Robertson. Sam Houston was one of the shareholders. He was preparing to make his first campaign for congress at the time.

58

59

58) Robertson County got its name from a colony founded by a syndicate of speculators from Tennessee. Sterling C. Robertson took the lead in bringing settlers to the colony, established in 1826. He was born in Tennessee in 1785 and died in Texas in 1842.

59) One of the settlers Sterling Robertson brought here from Tennessee was his nephew George Childress. He was a lawyer and he got here just in time to get elected, along with Robertson, to represent the Robertson Colony at the Convention of 1836 at Washington-on-the-Brazos. George Childress wrote the Texas Declaration of Independence. He and Robertson were among the signers. So was Sam Houston, one of the early stockholders in the syndicate that established the Robertson Colony. The Mexicans never believed this was just a string of coincidences.

The Texas Associations's original plan was to apply for some land in Texas just to speculate with. The idea of a colony seems to have developed later. The Texas Association sent Robert Leftwich to Mexico City to apply for a grant of land. It took him about three years to get it because the Mexican congress transferred jurisdiction over colonial grants to the state governments while the negotiations were going on. Leftwich had to go to the capital of Coahuila and Texas at Saltillo and start all over.

Leftwich spent all the money the association had granted him before he accomplished his mission. He had to borrow money on his own account to pursue the project, so he had the grant put in his name when it finally came through. The Texas Association reimbursed him. The colony was known as the Nashville Colony for a time after that but eventually it came to be known as the Robertson Colony because the Robertsons led the effort to bring in settlers.

Felix and Sterling Robertson came to Texas in 1826 to survey the colony. Felix went back to Tennessee then to advertise for colonists. Sterling Robertson stayed here to supervise and tell the settlers where to settle.

Relations between Robertson and Stephen F. Austin got a little strained in 1830 after the Mexican congress adopted a law against further colonizing by Anglos. Only the old San Antonio Road separated the north end of Austin's colony from the south end of Robertson's colony. Austin had learned how to deal with the Mexican bureaucracy. He was able to persuade the authorities that he should be allowed to continue bringing settlers in because he was already doing it before the law was changed. Robertson asked Austin to intercede for him and make the same argument for the Robertson Colony. Austin interceded but he somehow got the whole Robertson Colony added to his own grant in the process. Robertson found out somebody was telling the Mexicans he had not brought in as many colonists as he was supposed to. Robertson suspected that somebody in the Austin camp was spreading that story.

Sterling Robertson made a trip to Mexico and came back with permission to continue bringing in settlers, and he got his colony back. One of the settlers arriving in the Robertson Colony shortly before Texans declared their independence was George Childress. He was one of Robertson's nephews from Tennessee. Robertson and Childress went to the Convention of 1836 at

60

60) The Cavitt house probably is the oldest surviving building in Wheelock. It was started in 1842 and completed in 1854. The Cavitts were friends of Sam Houston and it is said that General Houston stayed here several times.

61

61) Owensville lost the county seat to Calvert in 1870, but Calvert didn't keep it very long, either.

62

62) Franklin qualified in 1913 for one of the library buildings Andrew Carnegie was donating. Carnegie built the buildings but the communities he favored had to furnish the books and upkeep. Franklin couldn't afford many books and most of the library building was used as a school until 1984. The school district didn't need it any more, then, and the citizens of Franklin raised the money to restore the building as a library, fulfilling at last the city's promise to the Carnegie Foundation. Franklin has been the county seat since 1879.

63

63) Walter Williams was reputed to be 117 years old when he died in 1959. His family said Williams had served with the Confederate forces in the Civil War and he was recognized as the last survivor of that war before he died. Williams is buried in Mount Pleasant Cemetery at Franklin.

64

64) Hearne is the biggest town in Robertson County and one of the few that never has been the county seat. Hearne has several fine homes from the days when cotton was making some people here rich. This is the Philen house at 604 Magnolia.

65) Calvert flourished as a trade center until World War II. Most of the old buildings on the main street have since been turned into antique shops. Calvert once had the biggest cotton gin in the world.

Washington-on-the-Brazos as the representatives of the Robertson Colony. Childress wrote the Declaration of Independence they both signed there.

Stephen F. Austin's partner, Samuel M. Williams, persuaded the Mexicans to change their minds again and give the Robertson Colony back to him and Austin shortly before the colonists declared for independence. But the government of the Republic of Texas later ratified Robertson's claim and the grants he and his agents had made. Robertson served a term in the congress of the republic before he died in 1842.

The congress of the republic included all of the Robertson Colony and some additional land in the original Milam County, established in 1836. All of the original Milam County east of the Brazos River was split off in 1837 to form Robertson County. Parcels of the original Robertson County were later split off to make Leon, Limestone, and Freestone counties and parts of Madison, Brazos, and Falls counties. The present boundaries of Robertson County were fixed in 1846. The county seat has changed five times.

The original county officials took office in a settlement called Franklin because it was about as important a town as there was in the area in 1837. The government moved in 1850 to Wheelock and stayed there until 1856. Then it moved to Owensville and stayed until 1870. The legislature ordered the county seat transferred to Calvert that year. The voters in the county elected, in 1879, to move the government to a new town on the International and Great Northern Railroad. The railroad had named the town Morgan. But the Post Office Department complained that there were too many towns named Morgan and the name was changed to Franklin. It was called New Franklin for a time, to distinguish it from the original county seat that was called Old Franklin until it disappeared.

New Franklin had been founded, as Morgan, in 1871 and named for a railroad official. Calvert was laid out by land speculators working with the Houston and Texas Central Railroad and named for landowner Robert Calvert. Hearne was also conceived by the railroad and named for landowner S. W.

66

66) One of Calvert's native sons went on to a successful political career on the West Coast. Los Angeles Mayor Tom Bradley was born in Calvert in 1917.

Hearne. Bremond was named for H&TC president Paul Bremond. Old Franklin and Owensville have disappeared. Wheelock is still on the map.

This was part of the original Texas cotton belt. There were big plantations here before the Civil War and cotton continued to be a very important crop into the 20th century. Planters hired some Chinese laborers after the slaves were set free. The Chinese had come to Texas originally to work on the railroads. Some of them settled here. Calvert once had the biggest cotton gin in the country. Most of the agricultural income now comes from livestock and poultry but farmers here still produce some cotton, grains, and watermelons. There is a little oil and gas.

Falls County _____

The Caddo, Waco, and Anadarko Indians lived here before the Spanish laid claim to Texas and the Comanches were ranging over the area by the time the first settlers got here. There were no Spanish or Mexican settlements. The first Anglos in what is now Falls County were members of the Robertson Colony. Sterling Robertson established his headquarters here, on the west bank of the Brazos, in 1834.

Robertson named his first settlement Sarahville de Viesca. Sarah was Robertson's mother's name. Agustin de Viesca was the governor of the Mexican state of Coahuila and Texas at the time. Relations between Viesca and the Anglo colonists evidently were pretty good. Viesca once tried to move the state capital to Texas, as a means of settling a dispute over whether it should be in Saltillo or Monclova.

Robertson chose the location for his headquarters settlement because it was near a natural crossing on the Brazos. The river was a major obstacle to

67) Falls County was named for a natural landmark that was both conspicuous and useful in the early days. The Brazos River tumbles over a shallow rock ledge here. The rock bottom above the falls made a convenient ford. There is a small county park beside the falls just south of Marlin.

travelers in the early days but the Indians had learned that the river could be forded handily by following a rock outcrop that created a modest waterfall the settlers came to refer to as the Falls of the Brazos. The rock provided the firm footing for hooves and wheels that was lacking in most stretches of the river. The Brazos has changed course some and the flow has been altered by various dams. The drop at the falls is said to have been ten feet once. It is about two feet now.

The settlement at Sarahville did not last long. It was very vulnerable to Indian attacks. Settlers abandoned the whole area here during the Runaway Scrape after the fall of the Alamo in the spring of 1836. John Marlin and his family were the first settlers to return after the Mexicans were defeated at San Jacinto. The Marlins settled on the east bank of the Brazos, opposite Sarahville. Their settlement was called Bucksnort and it had the first post office in the area.

The legislature took part of Limestone County and part of Milam County to create a new county in 1850. The new county was named for the falls and Sarahville was designated the county seat. But the government moved to the east bank of the river less than a year later and set up shop near Bucksnort in a settlement called Adams Spring because it had been established by Allensworth Adams. The name of the settlement was changed almost immediately to Marlin in honor of John Marlin. Marlin has been the county seat of Falls County ever since.

68

69

68) *People don't have as much faith in the efficacy of hot mineral water as they once did, but there is plenty of it available, free, in Marlin. The water feeding this public fountain comes from the original hot well, discovered in 1891.*

69) *The bath houses did a big business in Marlin into the 1930s. Conrad Hilton built one of his early hotels here. It is vacant now, and the surviving bathhouses are, too.*

70

70) *Marlin banker B. C. Clark built this mansion in 1900 and lived here until he killed himself in 1915. His widow moved away in 1923 and the big house was deteriorating when the Lee Loefflers bought it and restored it. The Thomas Michalskys bought it from the Loefflers in 1970 and they have it open for tours daily. SH 6 at FM 147. Fee.*

Indians harrassed the settlers here for several years after Texas won independence from Mexico. There was an attack in 1839 on the home the John Marlins and the George Morgans were sharing. The Marlins all survived the attack. Morgan and his wife and two other settlers were killed. John Marlin's daughter Stayce was beaten and left for dead but she recovered.

The settlers set out to punish the raiders. They caught up with the Indians on the west bank of the Brazos. The Indians pretended to retreat and set up an ambush. They killed ten of the settlers but Indian Chief Jose Maria was injured in the fight. He lived to see his Anadarkos confined later to the Brazos Indian Reservation and then to the Oklahoma Indian Territory.

71

71) A local politician started an important career in national politics with this parade in Marlin in 1916. Tom Connally had been a soldier and a member of the legislature and county attorney before he made his run for the U.S House of Representatives. He was elected and the first vote he cast as a congressman was in favor of declaring war on Germany in 1917.

72

72) Tom Connally moved up to the Senate in 1928. He became one of the most powerful members of that body and chaired the Senate Foreign Relations Committee during World War II. Connally retired from the Senate in 1952. He died in Washington in 1963 and was buried in Marlin.

Marlin got a boost when the Houston and Texas Central Railroad reached here in 1871. A crew drilling a water well for the city in 1891 tapped unexpectedly into a pool of hot mineral water. The hot well and the railroad soon turned Marlin into a health resort. The last of the public baths closed years ago but there is still plenty of hot water and some people still drink it.

109

73) German immigrants settled Westphalia in 1879. The first church they build was destroyed by a storm in 1884. The present Catholic Church of the Visitation was built the same year. It is one of the biggest frame churches in Texas.

73

The population of Falls County grew to about 35,000 by 1940 but it is only a little more than half that now. Marlin is the biggest city. Rosebud was named for the rose bushes Mrs. J. L. Mullins brought with her when she settled here. The settlement had earlier been called Mormon. The settlement moved and the name was changed when the San Antonio and Aransas Pass Railroad came through in 1889. Chilton was established in the 1870s and called Abney until the San Antonio and Aransas Pass Railroad made it a station. It was renamed then for Frank Chilton. Reagan was established when the Waco and Northwest Railroad came through in 1873, and named for W. R. Reagan because he donated the site for the town. Lott was established by the San Antonio and Aransas Pass Railroad and named for railroad president Uriah Lott.

Cotton was the important factor in the economy of Falls County up until the early 20th century. Some cotton is grown here still, but livestock and poultry account for most of the farm income now. There is some manufacturing and a little oil and gas.

Bell County

Indians of the Caddo, Kickapoo, Comanche, and other tribes had their way here during the Spanish and Mexican rule and vigorously resisted Anglo settlement. The present Bell County was part of the Robertson Colony. A few colonists tried to settle along the Little River in 1834. They left during the panic following the fall of the Alamo and the Comanche attack on Fort Parker in 1836. A few came back after the panic subsided but the Indians ran them off in 1838. A ranger company led by John Bird clashed with a band of Indians here in the spring of 1839. The rangers won the fight but Bird was killed and settlers were not encouraged. There was no serious attempt at settlement again until 1843 and there were sporadic Indian attacks for another 15 years after that. The stream where Bird's rangers and the Indians fought has been known as Bird's Creek ever since.

75

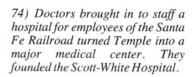

74

76

77

74) *Doctors brought in to staff a hospital for employees of the Santa Fe Railroad turned Temple into a major medical center. They founded the Scott-White Hospital.*

75) *The railroads' contribution to Temple's growth is remembered at the Railroad and Pioneer Museum at 710 Jack Baskin Street in Temple. But the depot here is not the Temple depot. It was brought in from Moody. Open Tuesday through Saturday 1 pm to 4 pm. Fee.*

76) *This old house at 518 North 7th Street in Temple once was the home of two governors of Texas. James and Miriam Ferguson lived here. He was elected governor in 1914 and impeached in 1917. But Jim Ferguson continued to be a factor in Texas politics during the two terms Mrs. Ferguson later served in the governor's office.*

77) *The county seat has been in Belton since Bell County was organized in 1850. The city and the county were named for Governor Peter Hansboro Bell. His statue stands on the courthouse grounds. The courthouse was built in 1885.*

The legislature took part of Milam County in 1850 to create this county. It was named for Peter Hansborough Bell. He was governor at the time. Bell came to Texas from Virginia in 1835. He fought at San Jacinto and served in the U.S. Army in the war with Mexico. He went from the governor's office to congress and represented Texas in the U.S. House until he decided to move to North Carolina in 1857. The Texas Legislature had Bell's remains brought

78

78) *This monument on the grounds of Mary Hardin Baylor University in Belton was built with stones from the first building built after this school moved here. Mary Hardin Baylor was originally the female department of Baylor University. It moved here from Independence when the men's department moved to Waco in 1887. The name was changed to Mary Hardin Baylor in 1934, after Mrs. Mary Hardin made a substantial gift to the school. The building these stones came from was Luther Hall, named for John Hill Luther. He was the first president to serve the school at this location. The monument is a tribute to him. Mary Hardin Baylor is the oldest women's university west of the Mississippi, but it is now coeducational.*

79

79) *Bell County's new Exposition Center is conspicuously located on I-35 in Belton. The center was completed in 1987.*

to Texas and buried in the State Cemetery in Austin after he died in North Carolina in 1898. Part of the original Bell County was taken away in 1856 to become Coryell County.

The voters of the new Bell County decided in 1850 to put the county seat near the center of the county at a place then called Nolan Springs. The name was changed to Nolanville and then changed to Belton. The early settlers mostly claimed lands along the streams and Bell County has a good supply of streams. Belton is near the junction of Nolan Creek and the Leon River. The Lampasas River and the Leon join in southern Bell County to form the Little River. These streams are part of the Brazos drainage system.

Salado Creek in southern Bell County attracted some of the early settlers. Elijah Sterling Clack Robertson was one of them. He was the son of the Robertson Colony's head man Sterling Clack Robertson. The younger Robertson was 12 years old when he came to Texas with his father in 1832. He later served in the Texas Army and became chief justice of Bell County after he settled on Salado Creek in 1852.

Elijah Robertson donated 100 acres of land to help establish Salado College in 1859 and the college made the settlement of Salado a town. The college operated until 1885. Salado was on the stage line from Austin and it was second only to Belton in importance until the railroads came and bypassed Salado. The town and the college were named for the creek. It was named by the early Spanish explorers but they probably meant the name for the Lampasas River and some cartographer transposed the names. Salado is the Spanish word for salty, which the Lampasas is and Salado Creek is not. This is not the creek where the Battle of Salado Creek was fought in 1842. That one is in Bexar County. There actually are four creeks in Texas named Salado.

The Gulf, Colorado, and Santa Fe was the first railroad to reach Bell County, in 1880. The railroad company wanted a bonus for running the tracks through Belton. The people of Belton agreed to the bonus and got a railroad station, but the Gulf, Colorado, and Santa Fe decided to put its division

80

81

80) There were seven grist mills on Salado Creek in Bell County in the late 1800s. Only two are left and they are no longer working mills. This is the old Summers Mill on FM 1123. It has been rebuilt twice because of flood damage, and it is now a guest house. It is privately owned.

81) Elijah S. C. Robertson built this plantation home at Salado in 1856. He was the son of Robertson Colony founder Sterling Robertson. This house is still in the Robertson family. Liz Carpenter was born here. She was a White House aide during the Johnson administration. Her mother was a Robertson.

82

83

82) Elijah Robertson helped establish Salado College in 1860. The school made Salado a town of some importance, while it lasted. The college closed in 1885 and the buildings are now in ruins.

83) The Stagecoach Inn in Salado was established by W. B. Armstrong in 1852. Robert E. Lee and George Custer stayed here. The inn was close to falling down in 1943 when Mr. and Mrs. Dion Van Bibber bought it and restored it and added a modern motel behind it. The Van Bibbers are gone now, but the restaurant they put in the original building, and the motel they added are still in businesses.

headquarters in a new town it created and named for railroad man B. M. Temple. The railroad jobs in the new town produced a lot of growth. The Missouri, Kansas, and Texas put a line through Temple in 1882 and by 1884 Temple was bigger than Belton.

The Santa Fe established a hospital for its employees in Temple and brought Dr. A. C. Scott and Dr. R. R. White in to run it. The doctors left the railroad hospital and started the Kings' Daughters' Hospital in 1889 and then founded the Scott-White Hospital in 1904. They made Temple a major medical center. But Temple is no longer the biggest town in the county. Killeen is a little larger and growing faster.

Killeen was established about 1882 and originally called Palo Alto. It was renamed for railroad man Frank Killeen when the Gulf, Colorado, and Santa Fe came through. Killeen gained some importance as a shipping point but its real growth began in 1942 when the U.S. Army established a base nearby to train crews for tank destroyers. The base was called Camp Hood in honor of Confederate General John Bell Hood. It became Fort Hood in 1946. It has grown into one of the biggest military bases in the world and Killeen is the gateway to Fort Hood.

84) The Central Texas Area Museum sponsors the Annual Gathering of the Scottish Clans and Highland Games in Salado each November with plenty of bagpipes.

84

The black land of eastern Bell County has produced a lot of cotton over the years. Farmers here still grow cotton and grains but livestock and poultry bring in more money than the crops. There have been no significant discoveries of oil or gas.

Museums

Belton

Bell County Museum. N. Main at 1st. 1 pm to 5 pm, Saturday and Sunday. Donations.

Salado

Central Texas Area Museum. Daily. Donations.

85

85) The U.S. Army Second Armored Division and First Cavalry Division both are based at Fort Hood. Both divisions have museums, open to the public. This is a portion of the Second Armored Museum.

115

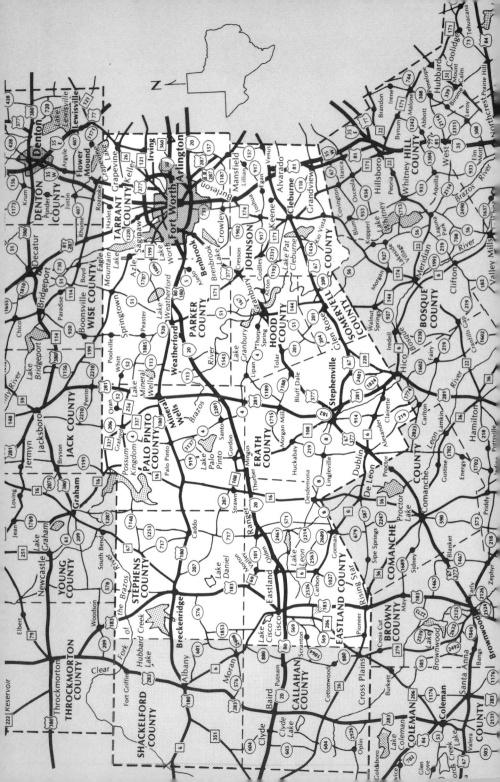

The Fort Worth Area

Tarrant, Johnson, Somervell, Hood, Erath,
Eastland, Stephens, Palo Pinto, and Parker ¯counties.

Indians of many tribes occupied this part of Texas when the republic was established in 1836. President Mirabeau Lamar sent General Edward H. Tarrant and the Texas Militia on a couple of punitive expeditions into the area in 1840 and 1841.

Sam Houston returned to the president's office at the end of 1841 and reversed Lamar's Indian policy. Houston sent word to the Indians here that they had a friend in the president's office again. He invited the Indian chiefs to meet with him at a little ranger fort Jonathan Bird had established on the West Fork of the Trinity.

Most of the tribes were represented when Houston appeared at Bird's Fort in August of 1843. The president spoke words the Indians wanted to hear and after he left General Tarrant and G. W. Terrell signed a treaty with the Indians. The treaty established a line running approximately through the present city of Fort Worth, through Menard to San Antonio. The parties all agreed that settlers would not intrude west of this line and the Indians would make no trouble east of the line. The congress of the republic ratified this treaty but there were wholesale violations on both sides. Whites claimed land and built cabins west of the treaty line. Indians raided homesteads and stole horses on both sides of the line.

This was the situation when Texas joined the Union at the end of 1845. It was the reason the U.S. Army started building forts along the frontier. Fort Worth was one of the first forts.

Tarrant County

This part of Texas was inhabited only by Indians until after the Texas Revolution succeeded and the Republic of Texas was established. The present Tarrant County was included in the land grants the Republic of Texas made in the early 1840s to W. S. Peters and his associates.

The first serious Anglo intrusion here was in May of 1841. A force of about 70 rangers and volunteers led by Edward H. Tarrant attacked three Indian villages on Village Creek. The Texans easily overran two of the villages but the Indians in the third village put up a vigorous fight. The Texans withdrew, but the Indians did, too, and the Texans were inspired to try to establish a permanent presence in the neighborhood. They built a small block-house and stockade near the West Fork of the Trinity River about seven miles north of the present city of Arlington. A small party of rangers commanded

2

1, previous page) The Will Rogers Coliseum on West Montgomery has been the home of the Fort Worth Stock Show and Rodeo since the 1940s. The Coliseum was named for the late cowboy humorist from Oklahoma at the suggestion of his friend Amon Carter.

2) Fort Worth tried for years to compete with Dallas in everything but fashion. Fort Worth even built a big airport to compete with Love Field but it was not a success and ultimately the two cities got together to build the huge Dallas-Fort Worth Airport (DFW). The name of Dallas precedes the name of Fort Worth, but the terminals are in Tarrant County. The airport straddles the county line north of Arlington.

3

3) *Arlington is one of the fastest-growing cities in Texas, and it has one of the top tourist attractions. Six Flags Over Texas was one of the nation's early big-league amusement parks. Six Flags is open daily in the summer; weekends in the spring and fall. Fee.*

4

4) *The University of Texas at Arlington went through a series of name changes between 1895 when it was founded as Arlington College and 1967 when it became part of the University of Texas System.*

by Jonathan Bird occupied Bird's Fort for about a year and then abandoned it. A few setttlers showed up about the same time and camped around Bird's Fort, but not for long. They soon moved east to John Neely Bryan's settlement at what was to become the city of Dallas. The fort was idle until 1843 when President Houston used it for his meeting with the Indians.

The first permanent settlement in what is now Tarrant County was Lonesome Dove, where Grapevine is today. Lonesome Dove was established in 1845

5) The General Motors plant at Arlington assembles the company's rear-wheel-drive models.

6) Traders' Village in Grand Prairie is said to have been the first flea market designed and built for this purpose. It's been open weekends since 1973. There is an RV park adjacent to it. 2602 Mayfield Road, near the I-20/360 interchange. There is a parking fee but no charge for admission to the village.

6

by a party of immigrants from Missouri. The Lonesome Dove church, organized in 1846, was the first in what is now Tarrant County.

The Peters Colony grants generated a great deal of controversy and a couple of lawsuits and the grantees had only settled about 150 people in the area that is now Tarrant County when the Peters grant expired in 1848. The area had been included in Navarro County when the legislature created Navarro County in 1846. The legislature divided Navarro County in 1849 and created this county, naming it for Edward H. Tarrant. He had come to Texas from Tennessee in 1835. Tarrant was a member of the legislature by the time this county was organized. He died at Fort Belknap in 1858 and his remains are buried in the Pioneer Rest Cemetery in Fort Worth.

Two men destined to play big roles in shaping the future of Tarrant County came here in 1849 from opposite directions. Major Ripley Allen Arnold of the U.S. Army arrived from San Antonio at the head of a small force of dragoons with orders to establish an outpost to protect the frontier. Middleton Tate Johnson came from Shelby County in East Texas. He had been a member of the congress of the republic and he served with the Texas Rangers. Johnson got here a little bit ahead of Major Arnold. Johnson established a homestead he called Johnson Station near the present city of Arlington. This was a ranger

7

7) *Arlington Baptist College on US 80 has a fence, gate, and guardhouse. The guardhouse is not used now but it was quite necessary when this site was known as Top of the Hill Terrace. That was in the 1920s and '30s. Top of the Hill was a speakeasy and gambling resort. There were some high rollers in Arlington, then, attracted by the Arlington Downs racetrack where betting was then legal. Arlington Baptist College was chartered in 1939 as Fundamental Baptist Bible Institute. The school moved to this site in 1956.*

8

8) *Anglers flocked to Joe Pool Lake when it was opened to the public in 1989. The new lake straddles the Tarrant-Dallas County line between Grand Prairie and Cedar Hill. It was built by the Army Corps of Engineers to control flooding and supply water. It was named for the late Congressman Joe Pool.*

9

9) *The man Fort Worth was named for never saw the place. General William Jenkins Worth was commander of U.S. troops in Texas and New Mexico when he died shortly before Major Ripley Arnold established an outpost on the Trinity and gave it Worth's name.*

121

10) The first cemetery in Fort Worth was established in 1850 when two of Major Ripley Arnold's children died. Major Arnold himself was buried in Pioneers' Rest Cemetery after he was murdered at Fort Graham in 1953. General Edward Tarrant and many other early settlers are buried in the old cemetery in the 600 block of Samuels Street on the near northeast side of Fort Worth.

station and later a stage station. Johnson was the man Arnold consulted about a location for the outpost he was to establish. Johnson steered the major to a site he happened to own, on a bluff overlooking the junction of the Clear Fork and the West Fork of the Trinity River.

Arnold and his men called the post they built on the bluff Camp Worth, in honor of the general then commanding U.S. forces in Texas and New Mexico. General William Jenkins Worth was a veteran of the War of 1812 and the Mexican War and a native of New York State. He was dead of cholera by the time the camp here was established. The army changed the name from Camp Worth to Fort Worth about the time the first buildings were completed.

The biggest settlement within the county's boundaries when Tarrant County was created was Birdville, founded by William and Ben Ayers and named for Jonathan Bird. The legislature specified in creating the county that Birdville was to be the county seat. The original county government was established in Birdville. People by this time had started settling around Fort Worth too, and those settlers stayed when the troops moved from Fort Worth to Fort Belknap in 1853, as the frontier moved westward.

The army never had owned the land Fort Worth was built on. M. T. Johnson still owned it. He started selling the property to settlers after the troops departed. A few people took up residence in the old barracks buldings. One of the army buldings was turned into a store. All the original buildings were made of logs, and none survives.

The settlement at the former fort had a school and a post office by 1856. The mail was arriving and leaving on stage coaches operating between Dallas and Fort Belknap, along a road that is still called Belknap Street. The settlement adopted the name of the fort and by 1856 Fort Worth boosters had convinced themselves theirs was the coming town in Tarrant County. They decided Fort Worth should be the county seat and they promoted an election. The vote was in favor of moving the government from Birdville to Fort Worth but people in Birdville complained that voters from outside the county helped Fort Worth win. They managed to get a new election ordered but the second vote was not held until 1860. The government was already in Fort Worth by then and many former residents of Birdville had moved to Fort Worth. Fort Worth won the second election handily. Birdville was already dying.

Fort Worth became an important stage stop in the early 1860s. The Butterfield Line between Missouri and California did not pass through here, but it did make a stop at Jacksboro, to the northwest. Travelers from East Texas and the southeastern United States came to Fort Worth to catch the stage that connected with the Butterfield Line at Jacksboro. Fort Worth was the busiest stage terminal in the southwest for a few years immediately after the Civil War.

The vote on seceding from the Union in 1861 was fairly close in this county but people in favor of staying with the union were careful about what they

11

11) Ten million Texas cattle were driven to market in Kansas and elsewhere between 1866 and the 1890s. Many of them came through Fort Worth and crossed the Trinity River near the present North Main viaduct. This was the route of the Chisholm Trail.

12

12) The cattle-drive days are commemorated by a life-size sculpture outside the old stockyards on the north side of Fort Worth. The city's growth has not been in this direction in recent years, but Ross Perot, Jr. is working on a new development to the north including a vast industrial airport, so the Fort Worth growth pattern is likely to change.

14

15

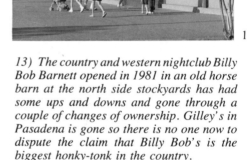

13

16

13) The country and western nightclub Billy Bob Barnett opened in 1981 in an old horse barn at the north side stockyards has had some ups and downs and gone through a couple of changes of ownership. Gilley's in Pasadena is gone so there is no one now to dispute the claim that Billy Bob's is the biggest honky-tonk in the country.

14) Fort Worth was one of the greatest cattle markets in the world when the Livestock Exchange building was built on Exchange Avenue in 1902.

15) The effort to develop the stockyards district into a tourist resort has not been an overwhelming success, but it continues. The Fort Worth Fat Stock Show and Rodeo started here but it outgrew the district and moved years ago. Fort Worth claims to have had the world's first indoor rodeo, in 1918.

16) The Will Rogers Coliseum occupies part of the site where Fort Worth celebrated the Texas Centennial in 1936 and 1937. The official celebration was in Dallas, but Fort Worth put on a rival show. The centerpiece was an outdoor supper theater with a floating stage and a musical review staged by Broadway producer Billy Rose.

17) *The Fort Worth Centennial celebration and the Casa Manana were promoted by Amon G. Carter. Carter was born in Crafton, Texas, in 1879. He came to Fort Worth in 1905 and went to work for* The Star *newspaper. He bought the paper in 1908 and renamed it the* Fort Worth Star Telegram. *He put the motto "Where the West begins" on the front page and he was Fort Worth's biggest booster 'til he died in 1955.*

17

18) *Carter built Texas' first television station. It went on the air September 27, 1947 as WBAP-TV. It is known now as KXAS-TV and it's owned by one of the media chains.*

18

said in public. Secessionist vigilantes hanged a couple of Northerners here in September of 1860 for criticizing slavery.

There were some cotton plantations and some slaves in Tarrant County before the Civil War, so there was some economic disruption after the war. But Tarrant County did not suffer as much as some counties did. The end of the war brought on the period of the great cattle drives. Northerners were hungry for meat and they had plenty of money. Texas had a surplus of cattle. Cowmen found that an animal worth $5 in Texas could be sold for as much as $50 in Chicago. Hundreds of thousands of Texas cows were driven north to the rail heads in Missouri and Kansas between 1865 and 1876 when the first railroad reached Fort Worth.

The cattle trail generally known as the Chisholm Trail because it connected in the Oklahoma Territory with a trail blazed by Indian trader Jesse Chisholm passed right through Fort Worth. The merchants of Fort Worth sold supplies of all kinds to the trail drivers, coming and going. The town's claim to the title "cowtown" really dates, though, from the founding of the Livestock Exchange here in 1878, two years after the Texas and Pacific Railroad came through. The cattle business assumed even more importance when Armour and Swift both built major packing plants adjacent to the Fort Worth Stockyards

125

19

19) The trustees of the foundation Amon Carter established spent some of the money he left for a spectacular water garden designed by Phillip Johnson. Carter's only daughter Ruth took the lead in the decision to create this memorial, surrounded by a park that occupies altogether four-and-a-half blocks in downtown Fort Worth.

20

20) Amon Carter collected paintings and sculptures by Frederick Remington and Charles Russell for a number of years. He left his collection to the Amon Carter Museum of Western Art he provided for in his will. The museum grounds, overlooking the Fort Worth skyline, feature a trio of statues executed by John Moore in 1955 and titled "Upright Motives." 3501 Camp Bowie Blvd. Tuesday through Saturday, 10 am to 5 pm. Sunday 1 pm to 5:30 pm. Free.

in 1902. The "cowtown" title lingers but the packing business has been decentralized and Fort Worth is now just one of many places where beef is processed.

The town that began as a military post became an important military town again shortly before the United States entered World War I. Three airfields were established here to train pilots for the Royal Canadian Air Force, many of them actually U.S. citizens. Hicks Field, Barron Field, and Carrothers Field began training pilots for the U.S. Army as soon as the United States

126

21

21) *Kay Kimbell started a milling company and expanded it into a vast network of corporations. He and his wife Velma amassed an outstanding art collection and created the Kimbell Art Foundation to provide an appropriate place for the collection after they died. The Kimbell Art Museum off West Montgomery in west Fort Worth was designed by Louis I. Kahn. It has been hailed as the finest small museum in the country. Tuesday through Saturday 10 am to 5 pm. Sunday 1 pm to 5 pm. Free.*

22

22) *The painting these people are contemplating in the Modern Art Museum of Fort Worth is "Stephen's Iron Crown"* by Robert Motherwell. This museum, too, is off West Montgomery in west Fort Worth. It and the Amon Carter and the Kimbell are within walking distance of each other. The Modern Art Museum started as an annex to the Carnegie Library in Fort Worth in 1901. It was known for many years as The Fort Worth Art Museum. Tuesday through Saturday 10 am to 5 pm. Sunday 1 pm to 5 pm. Free.*

entered the war in 1917. The 36th Division trained for World War I at the original Camp Bowie, west of Fort Worth, on what is still called Camp Bowie Boulevard. (The Camp Bowie where the 36th Divison trained for World War II was at Brownwood.)

Carswell Air Force Base was established in 1942 as Tarrant Field, between White Settlement and Lake Worth in western Tarrant County. The name of the base was changed to Carswell in 1948 to honor Major Horace Carswell of Fort Worth. He was killed in the fighting in China in 1944. General Dynamics builds warplanes next door to Carswell Air Force Base. Bell builds military helicopters in eastern Tarrant County.

Addison Clark came to Fort Worth in 1869 to establish a school for the Disciples of Christ. Addison moved to Hood County in 1874 to join his brother Randolph and their father in the operation of a college that eventually

---

* Museum purchase, Sid W. Richardson Foundation Fund, 1985.

23

24

25

26

23) The Forest Park Zoo in Fort Worth is an old one, started in 1909. Daily, 9 am to 5 pm. Fee.

24) The Fort Worth Botanic Garden has been expanded several times since it was established in Trinity Park in 1931. The rose garden here is the centerpiece. There also is a Fragrance Garden for the blind and a Japanese Garden. Open daily, 8 am to sundown. Free. The Japanese Garden is open Tuesday through Saturday 10 am to 5 pm and Sunday 1 pm to 5 pm and there is a fee.

25) Forest Park has a collection of seven restored log homes assembled in a village on University Drive. One of the houses has a working grist mill. Another once was the home of Isaac Parker, one of kidnap victim Cynthia Ann Parker's relatives. Monday through Friday 8 am to 4:30 pm and Saturday and Sunday afternoons. Fee.

26) Texas Christian University in Fort Worth got its start in Hood County as Add-Ran College in 1873. The school has been at the present site since 1911.

became Texas Christian University. Other institutions of higher learning in Tarrant County are the University of Texas at Arlington, Texas Weslayan College, Southwestern Baptist Theological Seminary, Texas College of Osteopathic Medicine, Arlington Baptist College, and Tarrant County Junior College.

Fort Worth has benefitted from the development of the West Texas oilfields but there is no oil production in the county. There is some gas. Agriculture

128

27

27) Butch Cassidy and the Wild Bunch came to Fort Worth in 1900 to celebrate after they robbed the First National Bank of Winnemuca, Nevada. They posed for this photograph in a Fort Worth studio and Cassidy (seated, right) sent a print with a note of thanks to the Nevada bank.

28

29

28) The Wild Bunch episode still echoes in downtown Fort Worth where a major redevelopment area is called Sundance Square for Cassidy's main sidekick. Heirs of the late oilman Sid Richardson developed Sundance Square.

29) The imposing Tarrant County Courthouse sits on the bluff above the Trinity on part of the site occupied by the army's original Fort Worth. The courthouse is pink granite. It was completed in 1893 and all the county commissioners were voted out of office at the next election. The voters thought the grand courthouse was an extravagance.

30

31

32

30) The depot the Santa Fe built in Fort Worth in the 1890s is still in use. The Amtrak trains stop here in the 1600 block of Jones.

31) One of the more extravagant homes built in Fort Worth during the cattle boom is Thistle Hill at 1509 Pennsylvania Avenue. Rancher W. T. Waggoner built it for his daughter Electra and her husband A. B. Wharton in 1903. Rancher Winfield Scott bought it in 1910. It has been restored and it is open for guided tours on weekdays from 10 am to 3:15 pm and on Sunday afternoons. Fee.

32) The late Edna Gladney of Fort Worth was an early champion of children's rights. Her campaign to find homes for the children of unwed mothers and stop the state practice of issuing birth certificates bearing the word "illegitimate" was dramatized in the 1942 MGM movie "Blossoms in the Dust" with Greer Garson.

33) The institution established in the 1890s as the Texas Children's Home and Aid Society was headed by Mrs. Gladney from 1925 'til 1960. The name was changed to Edna Gladney Home in 1950 to honor her. The home now is on Hemphill Street on the south side.

33

is not as important as it once was but there is substantial dairy farming and some ranching. Some cotton and grain crops are still grown. The population of about 1,000,000 is divided among about a dozen municipalities. Fort Worth has about one third of the county population and ranks as the fifth biggest city in Texas, behind Houston, Dallas, San Antonio, and El Paso.

Museum — Fort Worth

Cattleman's Museum. 1301 W. 7th. 8 am to 5 pm, Monday through Friday. Free.

34) General Dynamics builds warplanes at a plant next door to Carswell Air Force Base, on the south shore of Lake Worth. The Museum of Aviation near the General Dynamics main gate, off Spur 341 has several vintage airplanes on display. Open Wednesday through Saturday 10 am to 3 pm. Free.

34

Johnson County

Part of the area that is now Johnson County was included in the grant the Mexican government made to the Robertson Colony in 1827 and part was included in the grant the Republic of Texas made to the Peters Colony in 1841. Only Indians lived here until the 1840s. George Barnard was doing some trading with the Indians by that time. Henry Bridon settled here in 1849 near the present village of Rio Vista. He may have been the first settler.

The legislature created this county in 1854 by taking parts of Ellis, Hill, and Navarro counties. The county was named for the pioneer Tarrant County settler Middleton Tate Johnson. He was born in South Carolina. Johnson lived in Alabama and served in the legislature there before he came to Texas in 1840. He lived in Shelby County until 1849 when he moved to what is now Tarrant County and settled near what is now the city of Arlington. Johnson was very active in politics and he was an unsuccessful candidate for governor in 1851, three years before this county was created and named for him.

The few hundred people living here when the county was organized had some difficulty deciding where to put the county seat. There was an election in 1855 and the voters chose a site about five miles west of the present city

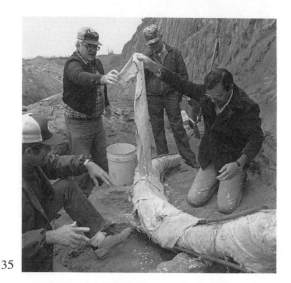

35

35) *Archaeologists uncovered this mammoth tusk in a gravel pit near Cleburne. It went into the Layland Memorial Museum in Cleburne.*

36

36) *The Layland Memorial Museum at 201 North Caddo Street occupies the old Carnegie Library Building. W. J. Layland was a plumbing contractor and amateur archaeologist. The museum exhibits are artifacts collected by him, plus some general Johnson County historical relics. Monday through Friday, 10 am to noon and 1 pm to 5 pm. Saturday 9 am to 1 pm. Free.*

of Cleburne. A town was laid out and named Wardville in honor of Thomas William Ward. He was serving as U.S. Consul in Panama at the time but Ward was a veteran of the Texas Revolution and he had been state land commissioner before he went to Panama. Ward County in West Texas was also named for Thomas William Ward. Ward County still exists, but Wardville has disappeared.

Somebody discovered that Wardville was not within five miles of the geographic center of the county as a county seat was then supposed to be. Another election was held and the county seat was moved to a settlement called Buchanan, about five miles northwest of the present city of Cleburne. Part of Johnson County was detached in 1866 to form Hood County. Buchanan was no longer at the center of what was left of Johnson County so there was

37

37) *Burleson is growing faster but Cleburne still is the biggest city in Johnson County. The present Johnson County Courthouse in Cleburne was built in 1912.*

38

38) *It sells no gas, but this replica of a 1920s gas station attracts a lot of attention to the adjacent auto body shop, on US 174, south of Cleburne.*

another election. That third vote put the county seat where it has been ever since. The site chosen was being called Camp Henderson at the time but the name was soon changed to Cleburne to honor the Confederate general Pat Cleburne. Johnson County was very strongly pro-Confederacy. The vote in favor of secession here in 1861 was about ten to one.

The first house in the settlement that became Cleburne was built in 1854 for Josephine Wren. The first railroad reached Cleburne in 1881. It was the Gulf, Colorado, and Santa Fe. The settlements of Burleson and Rio Vista became towns when the Gulf, Colorado, and Santa Fe came through. Joshua was founded in 1880 in anticipation of the railroad's arrival. Keene relocated to get on the rail line. Keene was settled in the 1850s by a Methodist family named Easterwood but it is now populated mostly by Seventh Day Adventists. Keene is the only town in Texas where most business establishments are closed on Saturdays and open on Sundays. Alvarado was named for the town

39

39) Henry Briden was one of the early settlers in Johnson County. He built this cabin near Rio Vista in 1849. Briden was a Texas Ranger. His cabin has been restored and moved to a site adjacent to the First State Bank of Rio Vista.

40

40) The First State Bank of Rio Vista advertises itself as the Cow Pasture Bank. The cow pasture adjacent to it is also a landing strip to accommodate customers traveling by plane.

41

41) The Cleburne State Recreation Area in the southwest corner of Johnson County is one of the state parks developed in the 1930s by the Civilian Conservation Corps. Off US 67, twelve miles southwest of Cleburne. Camping. Fee.

in Mexico because one of the early settlers had participated in the capture of Alvarado during the Mexican War. This Alvarado was settled about 1850.

Burleson is on the west leg of I-35 and growing because of its proximity to Fort Worth and Dallas. Part of Burleson is in Tarrant County. The town was settled before 1880 and named either for educator Rufus Burleson or San Jacinto hero Edward Burleson.

The river in western Johnson County that forms Lake Pat Cleburne is the Nolan, named for Philip Nolan. He was an early American adventurer and horse trader. Nolan made several trips into Spanish Texas between 1790 and 1800 ostensibly to capture wild horses. The Spanish always thought Nolan was an American spy and they killed him when they captured him in 1801. It is not certain where this happened but one theory is that it was here, near the river that now bears his name. But the name of the river is sometimes spelled Noland.

The economy of Johnson County was based originally on livestock and farming. Farms here still produce some cotton, peanuts, grains, and vegetables but the bulk of the agricultural income is from livestock. This is one of the state's leaders in dairy products. Many residents of Johnson County commute to jobs in Fort Worth.

Somervell County

Dinosaurs probably walked all over as much of Texas as was above sea level during their time on earth, but there are few places where the evidence is visible. Somervell County is one of those few places. The first footprints

42

42) The present Somervell County Courthouse in Glen Rose was built in 1893. A tornado wrecked the clock tower in 1902. The county fathers just boarded up the tower and left it that way until 1985. A major overhaul started then. It was completed in 1987. The exterior's been returned to its original appearance. The interior is all new.

43

43) The Somervell County Museum on the courthouse square has a collection of old photos, implements, furnishings, and fossils. Open Monday through Saturday, 10 am to 5 pm in the summer; weekends only in the winter. Free.

44

44) The town of Glen Rose developed around a mill and trading post George Barnard established on the Paluxy River in 1849. The old Barnard Mill was enlarged and converted to a sanitarium during the years when Glen Rose was a health resort. It is now a private residence.

to be identified as dinosaur tracks evidently were discovered in the bed of Wheeler Creek by George Adams about 1910. Charlie and William Moss found dinosaur tracks in the bed of the Paluxy River in 1934. Some of the tracks were cut out of the rock river bed and hauled off to the Museum of Natural History in New York before the Mosses and other citizens organized a campaign to preserve them. The citizens group obtained options on the land that eventually was incorporated into the Dinosaur Valley State Park, in 1969.

The Anadarko, Kichai, Tonkawa, and Comanche Indians roamed over this part of Texas without interference until 1859. The area had been included in the Robertson Colony but no settlements were attempted here during colonial days. L. B. McClanahan is said to have been the first settler in what is now Somervell County. He settled on the bank of the Paluxy and called his settlement Springtown because of the numerous natural springs in the vicinity. George Barnard established a trading post and mill in the same area later the same year and the place began to be called Barnard's Mill. Barnard had been a partner in the Torrey Trading House chain until he started trading with the

45

45) *Some imaginative rock work went into the design of the entrance building at Dinosaur Valley State Park on Park Road 59, off SH 205 west of Glen Rose. Camping. Fee.*

46

46) *Tracks like this were being cut out of the soft rock and hauled off to museums and private collections. Some of the dinosaur tracks in the Museum of Natural History in New York came from here.*

47

47) *The Fossil Rim Wildlife Ranch southwest of Glen Rose specializes in breeding and preserving endangered species of wildlife. It is open to visitors every day unless the weather is really bad. Fossil Rim is off US 67 about 3 miles southwest of Glen Rose.*

137

Indians on his own, about 1848. Other Anglos often complained that he was furnishing the Indians with whiskey and guns to the detriment of the general welfare, but Barnard also furnished supplies to the rangers and the army. Barnard's Mill got the first post office in the area in 1859.

The T. C. Jordans moved here from Dallas in 1870 and bought Barnard's Mill. Mrs. Jordan changed the name of the settlement to Glen Rose because of the wild roses growing in a glen near the mill.

The legislature took parts of Hood County and Johnson County to create this county in 1875. It was named for General Alexander Somervell although the name was spelled Somerville in the original legislation. Somervell was the officer chosen by President Sam Houston to command an expedition he sent to the Mexican border in 1842 to retaliate for two raids Mexican troops had made on San Antonio. Somervell's volunteers occupied Laredo and Guerrero briefly and then returned to Texas, except for about 300 men. Those 300 made the mistake of staying in Mexico to try to capture the town of Mier. The Mexicans captured them and executed some of them. Alexander Somervell was serving as a customs collector when he died in 1854.

Glen Rose has been the county seat from the beginning. One of the local legends concerns a character known when he lived here as John St. Helen. He lived in Hood County and Somervell County after the Civil War and he is said to have confessed when he was dying that he actually was President Lincoln's assassin, John Wilkes Booth.

Mineral springs made Glen Rose a health resort in the horse and buggy days and there are some resorts and summer camps here, still. The Comanche Peak nuclear power plant is a few miles north of the county seat. This is the second smallest county in Texas. Only Rockwell County is smaller in area. The population of Somervell County is under 5,000 and about half the county's residents live in Glen Rose. There is some ranching, a little farming, and no oil. Entertaining tourists is about the biggest business in Somervell County.

48

48) The new presence in Somervell County is the Comanche Peak Nuclear Power Plant north of Glen Rose off SH 201. The Squaw Creek Reservoir created to provide cooling water straddles the Somervell-Hood County line. There is a Visitor Center.

Hood County

The Kiowa and Comanche Indians were in complete and unchallenged control of this part of Texas until several years after Texas joined the United States. There were no serious attempts at settlement until about 1854. Thomas Lambert and Amon Bond were among the first settlers. Lambert settled at what is now the town of Granbury. Bond started a settlement nearby and called it Stockton, but he later moved to Granbury.

Davy Crockett's widow Elizabeth and their son Robert were early settlers in Hood County. Mrs. Crockett was entitled to the land grant Crockett earned serving in the Texas Army at the Alamo, but she did not come to Texas until 1855. Much of the land had been claimed by then and Elizabeth Crockett had to sign half her grant over to the surveyor who found the property she claimed here, north of the present city of Granbury.

Pleasant Thorp settled at a mineral spring near the Brazos River in 1855 and started the community that became Thorp Spring.

The legislature took part of Johnson County in 1866 to create this county. It was a time when southerners were busy naming streets, schools, towns, and counties for the heroes of the war they had just lost. This county was named for one Confederate general and the county seat was named for another one.

The county was named for John Bell Hood. He was not a native Texan, but Texans were proud to have his name associated with their state. Hood was born in Kentucky. He went to West Point and served with the army in

49) Mrs. Davy Crockett stayed home in Tennessee with their children when Davy came to Texas to fight the Mexicans. Davy earned a land grant for serving at the Alamo. Mrs. Crockett came to Texas in 1855 to claim the land. She ended up with a tract in Hood County and lived here 'til she died in 1860. Elizabeth Crockett's grave in the cemetery at Acton is maintained by the Texas Parks and Wildlife Department. It is the smallest state park in Texas.

49

139

50) The town of Granbury was built on the bank of the Brazos River. The Brazos River Authority built a dam in the 1960s which created a lake on Granbury's doorstep. The lake brought a lot of new people to town and some new money. The newcomers played a large role in the restoration of the courthouse and the surrounding buildings.

50

51

52

51) The 1886 Opera House was in ruins in 1960. It's in good condition now and presenting programs again.

52) The Nutt House was a store in the 1890s. There is a restaurant, now, downstairs, and a hotel upstairs. Bus tour conductors are partial to Granbury. A number of people commute from here to jobs in Fort Worth.

Missouri and California before he was transferred to Texas in 1856. He served at several army posts in Texas until 1861, when he resigned to accept a commission in the Confederate Army. Hood was placed in command of the Fourth Texas Infantry and he soon was promoted to commander of the brigade the regiment was attached to. He went on to higher commands but the brigade retained his name throughout the war and distinguished itself in numerous engagements.

53   54

53) The actor blamed for killing President Abraham Lincoln supposedly was trapped and killed in a barn in Virginia twelve days later. But a local legend holds that John Wilkes Booth really escaped and lived for a while in Granbury as John St. Helen before he moved to Glen Rose and disappeared.

54) Texas Christian University started here, at Thorp Spring, in Hood County. The original name was Add-Ran College. A couple of other schools operated in the old Add-Ran buildings after Add-Ran moved to Waco in 1902. The last one was Thorp Spring Christian College. It closed in 1930 and Thorp Spring was about to die before Lake Granbury brought in some new people.

The legislature decreed that the county seat of Hood County had to be named Granbury. But the lawmakers got the spelling wrong, as they often did. The man they were determined to honor was Hiram B. Granberry. He had been a lawyer and judge in Waco before the Civil War began. He joined the Seventh Regiment of Texas Infantry as a captain, and rose to brigadier general. Granberry was commanding Hood's Texas Brigade in a battle at Franklin, Tennessee, when he was killed, in 1864. His remains were brought here and buried in the town named for him.

The Hood County Courthouse burned in 1875 and most of the county records were destroyed, so there is some uncertainty about the details. But it evidently took about three elections to decide where the county seat would be located. The location finally chosen was the settlement Thomas Lambert had started in 1854. Lambert, J. F. Nutt, and J. Nutt donated 40 acres of land for the townsite, on the west bank of the Brazos, near the center of the county.

141

Two colleges were established in Hood County in 1873. The Methodists started Granbury College in Granbury and operated it until 1889. Sam Milliken in the meantime had bought part of Pleasant Thorp's land and he and Thorp developed a little health resort at Thorp Spring. They wanted their town to have a school so they built a school building. Elder J. A. Clark of the Disciples of Christ came along and made arrangements to take over the building. Clark and his sons Addison and Randolph started a college they called Add-Ran College. It was a private school until the Clarks gave it to the Disciples of Christ. The church changed the name to Add-Ran Christian University and built some new buildings. But Thorp Spring never got rail service. Enrollment was declining when church officials decided in 1895 to move Add-Ran Christian to Waco. The name was changed from Add-Ran to Texas Christian University in 1902. And T.C.U. moved to Fort Worth after a fire destroyed the main building on the Waco campus in 1911.

The Fort Worth and Rio Grande Railroad reached Granbury in 1887. Thorp Spring was once a stop on the stage line between Fort Worth and Yuma. But only one U.S. highway passes through Hood County and it has never been very heavily traveled. Hood County was a quiet place and Granbury was a declining country town when the Brazos River Authority decided in the 1960s to build a dam at De Cordova Bend. The dam created Lake Granbury. The lake brought in visitors and new residents, subdivisions, and money.

The new people thought the little stone courthouse and the stone store buildings around the square were quaint. They began to buy them and restore them. The square and nine blocks of downtown Granbury are now listed in the National Register of Historic Places.

There is a little irrigation here and farmers produce grains and peanuts. More than half the agricultural income is from livestock. There has been some drilling, but Hood County has never had an oil strike.

Erath County

This area was inhabited by nomadic Indians from before the time the Spanish first became aware of it until the 1870s. What is now Erath County was part of the Robertson Colony after 1827, but the presence of the hostile Indians discouraged settlement until the 1850s. John and William Stephen and about 30 other pioneers settled here in 1854. The Stephen brothers started the first store and the settlement was called Stephenville. John Stephen donated the town site and some additional land to encourage the legislature to make his town the county seat when Erath County was created from parts of Bosque and Coryell counties in 1856. The county was named for George B. Erath. He came to Texas from Austria in 1833 and got a job as a surveyor for the Robertson Colony. He made the original survey of John Stephen's town. Erath fought at San Jacinto and served in the congress of the republic and in the legislature after annexation.

Indian attacks caused some of the settlers in Erath County to leave during the Civil War. The frontier moved backwards during that period and Indian attacks continued off and on into the middle 1870s. H. G. Perry wrote in his book *Grand Ol' Erath* that most men were still wearing pistols to church in 1871. Perry quotes W. H. Fooshee as saying the first time he attended church in Stephenville, the preacher was armed, too. Stephenville was a stop on the stage line between Fort Worth and Yuma until the first railroad arrived in 1890. Dublin was the first town in the county to get rail service.

A. H. Dobkins founded the town that became Dublin in 1854. The name was not adopted until 1860. The town was not named for the Irish city. It is said that the spelling originally was Doublin and that it derived from the settlers' custom of doubling up, joining forces, to defend their homes against Indian attacks.

The Houston and Texas Central Railroad laid tracks into southern Erath County in 1881 and offered to bring the line through Dublin if the city would put up a bonus. The people of Dublin declined the offer. The railroad laid its tracks to miss Dublin by three or four miles. The railroad created a new

55

55) Tarleton State University was established in 1893 as Stephenville College. It became John Tarleton College in 1898, was annexed to the Texas A&M System in 1917, and raised to university status in 1958.

56

56) The old J. C. Berry house at 525 East Washington is the oldest house in Stephenville. It was built in 1869. It is now a museum. Open Tuesday through Sunday, 2 pm to 5 pm.

57) *The Dublin Historical Society maintains a small museum in one of the oldest commercial buildings in downtown Dublin. The building at 113 East Blackjack was built in 1880. Open Saturdays 2 pm to 4 pm.*

57

58) *The flour and grist mill William Miller built in Dublin in 1882 is also owned by the Dublin Historical Society. The mill continued to make cattle and chicken feed until 1974 when the last owner donated it to the society. It is used mostly for meetings. Most of the old machinery is still in place.*

58

town and named it Mount Airy. It was a station, but it didn't attract any settlers. The people of Dublin picked their town up and moved it to the railroad and the trains began stopping at Dublin.

There were some exceptions, but most Texas towns were anxious to get rail service during the railroad building boom. Many towns offered special inducements to the railroad companies. The inducements encouraged arrogance, and the arrogance produced the public resentment that produced the Texas Railroad Commission. The commission was established about ten years after the Dublin incident. It is known best today as the agency that regulates

59

59) *The formula for Dr. Pepper was developed in 1885 by a druggist in Waco. It was a fountain drink until 1891. Dr. Pepper was first put in bottles that year by the Dublin Bottling Company in Dublin. The plant is still operating and still bottling Dr. Pepper.*

the oil business, but the commission was established during Governor Jim Hogg's administration to rein in the railroads.

There are substantial coal deposits in this county. The coal mines at Thurber in northern Erath County were the most important in the state between the late 1880s and the early 1920s. W. W. and Harvey Johnson started the mines in 1886 to supply coal to the railroads. Labor troubles caused the Johnsons to sell out to the Texas Pacific Coal Company in 1888. Officials of the Texas Pacific named the town for one of their associates. They agreed to unprecedented labor contracts that made Thurber a 100% union town. But the coal company owned every building and all the businesses in Thurber.

The Texas Pacific Coal Company made the oil discovery that started the boom at Ranger, in the next county, in 1917. The company reorganized as the Texas Pacific Coal and Oil Company. The importance of coal declined as the railroads started using oil. The mines closed in 1921. Most of the people moved away. Most of the buildings were demolished or moved. Texas Pacific's Thurber brick plant continued to make paving bricks until 1930 when it closed, too. Thurber became a ghost town.

Huckaby, northwest of Stephenville, was known as Flatwoods until it was renamed for postmaster John Huckaby. Lingleville was named for early settler John Lingle. Morgan Mill took its name from John Morgan's sawmill.

Erath County has some manufacturing and a little oil. Cotton was the mainstay of the economy for 70 years but livestock and poultry are much more important, now. Only Hopkins County produces more milk.

Eastland County

The present Eastland County was part of the territory the Mexican government awarded to Stephen F. Austin and Samuel May Williams for colonizing purposes. But only the Tonkawa, Kiowa, and Comanche Indians lived here before the 1850s. The early settlers were Frank Sanchez and the William Manskers, C. C. Blairs, and James Ellisons. The Blair family settled near the Leon River in 1857. Blair put a stockade around his compound and the Blairs and several other pioneer families stood off the Indians and remained at Fort Blair throughout the Civil War when many other frontier residents were forced to move back eastward.

The Blair settlement became a stop on the stage line between Waco and Fort Griffin after the Civil War and eventually adopted the name Desdemonia. The Post Office Department shortened the name to Desdemona in 1901. The legislature created Eastland County in 1858 from part of Bosque, Coryell, and Travis counties. It was named for William Mosby Eastland. He was a veteran of the Battle of San Jacinto, executed by the Mexicans in 1843. Eastland was with a party of Texans making an unauthorized raid on the Mexican border town of Mier in December of 1842.

The census takers found only 99 people in Eastland County in 1860. They never counted Indians in those days. There were not enough settlers to justify a county government until 1873. A settlement named Merriman was designated the county seat when the government finally was organized that year. A persuasive settler from Kentucky named Charles Ulrich Connellee promoted an election and got the government moved in 1875 to the town he had founded the same year and named Eastland. Cisco is bigger, now, but Eastland is still the county seat.

Cisco was first called Red Gap and originally located about a mile west of the present location. The settlers moved in 1881 to get on the new Texas and Pacific rail line. The name Cisco is said to have been suggested by an official of the railroad. The settlement that became the city of Ranger grew up around

60) *The oil boom is just a memory in Ranger. Oil is still produced here but the lease hounds and the speculators left a long time ago. The population is down to about 3,000 from a high of 30,000 in the middle 1920s.*

60

61

61) Peanuts are a major factor in the agricultural economy of Eastland County. The peanuts are harvested in the fall and processed at a big plant the Birdsong Company operates at Gorman. About half the crop goes into peanut butter.

62

62) There is a legend that a horned toad sealed up in the cornerstone of the previous courthouse in 1897 was still alive when the cornerstone was opened in 1928. They take the legend seriously here. A little monument to the toad known as Old Rip is built into one of the walls of the present courthouse. Old Rip is said to have died about a year after he was taken out of the cornerstone.

63

63) Charles U. Connallee founded the city of Eastland. His house still stands at 575 South Lamar. The first floor was built in 1876 and the house was enlarged to its present size in 1924.

147

64

64) The late Conrad Hilton came to Eastland County in 1919 looking for a way to make some money from the oil boom. The few hotels here were doing good business and one of them was for sale so Hilton bought it.

65

65) The Mobley Hotel in Cisco was three years old when Hilton got it. He only operated it a few years and he never changed the name, but this was the original Hilton Hotel. It is now a community center.

a ranger camp and it was called Ranger Camp Valley until 1880 when the population moved two miles west to get on the Texas and Pacific line. The name of the town was shortened to Ranger in 1883. Rising Star was settled by six families from East Texas in 1876. They named it Rising Star because they thought crop prospects were so bright. Gorman was originally known as Shinoak and renamed for railroad man Pat Gorman when the Texas Central Railroad built its line through.

One of the most spectacular oil booms in Texas history happened here in Eastland County while the Arabs were still riding camels. W. K. Gordon and the Texas Pacific Coal Company brought in a gusher near Ranger on October 21, 1917. World War I was pushing up demand for oil. Leasehounds, drillers, and speculators swarmed in and expanded the Ranger Field to Desdemona and Breckenridge. The population of Ranger jumped from a few hundred to 16,000 by 1920 and reached 30,000 before the boom waned. Living space was so scarce at the height of the boom that homeowners were renting beds for eight hours at a time and even renting chairs to oilmen unable to find beds. More than 5,000 wells were drilled. Fortunes were made. There was no proration and no thought of conservation. The gas that came out of the ground with the oil was a nuisance that was flared off or allowed to blow away. Production declined sharply after the first two or three years because of the operators' ignorance and extravagance. But some wells here still produce oil and gas. Texas Pacific Coal Company became Texas Pacific Coal and Oil Company after the strike at Ranger. The company had thousands of acres under lease in the Ranger Field. The owners sold their holdings to the Seagrams whiskey people for $227,000,000 in 1963. Seagrams sold them to Sun Oil in 1980 for more than $2 billion.

The petroleum industry is still the biggest factor in the economy of Eastland County. There is some manufacturing and substantial ranching. About 10,000 acres of farmland are under irrigation in the county. The principal crops are peanuts, wheat, and feed grains. Gorman is a major peanut processing center.

Stephens County

No one disputed the Indians' control of this part of Texas until 1857. The first settler was John R. Baylor. He is said to have built a cabin that year on the Clear Fork of the Brazos. Baylor had been a member of the state legislature and he was an Indian agent for the state until Indian Superintendent Robert Neighbors fired him for opposing official policies. Baylor didn't like Indians. He led a party of settlers, after he was removed from the agent's office, in a skirmish with reservation Indians that caused the state to abandon the Indian

66) Some of the wells drilled within the city of Breckenridge during the boom are still producing oil. The bank building in the background here is the former Burch Hotel.

66

149

67   68

67) Some of the history of the oil boom is preserved in the J. D. Sandefer Annex of the Swenson Memorial Museum at 116 West Walker in downtown Breckenridge. The museum, in a retired bank building, has exhibits dealing mostly with the history of the area. It was named for pioneer ranchers Peter and Christina Swenson. The annex was named for oilman J. D. Sandefer. Tuesday through Saturday, 9 am to noon and 1 pm to 5 pm. Free.

68) Breckenridge has been the county seat since Stephens County was organized. The present courthouse was built during the oil boom, in 1926.

reservations in Throckmorton and Young counties in 1859. Baylor later served in the Confederate Army and Confederate Congress. He died in Montell in 1894.

Stephens County was created by the legislature in 1858 and the names of the county and the county seat reflect local opinion on what was the greatest issue of the period when the county was born. The county was first named Buchanan for James Buchanan. He was president of the United States at the time. But sentiment in favor of seceding from the United States was already growing in Texas. Abraham Lincoln had been elected president and Texans had voted to secede by 1861. The name of this county was changed then from Buchanan to Stephens, to honor Alexander Stephens. He was vice president of the Confederate States of America.

There was no need to change the name of the county seat. Breckenridge was named for John C. Breckinridge of Kentucky. He was vice president of the United States under Buchanan. But Breckinridge had excellent Southern credentials. He was the candidate the Secessionist Democrats chose to run for president in 1860 against the Republicans' Abraham Lincoln and the

150

Northern Democrats' Stephen Douglas. Breckinridge ran third in that race, but he carried Texas handsomely. Texans managed to misspell his name, though, when they named Breckenridge for him.

A village called Picketville was the temporary county seat here during the Civil War but no formal government had yet been established. The few settlers in the county huddled together in stockaded settlements at Picketville, Fort Davis, and Fort Mugginsville. Bands of Kiowa and Comanche Indians roamed the area but Stephens County was a little less subject to Indian raids than Shackelford County during the war.

The organization of the county government at Breckenridge was not accomplished until 1876. The Indians had been moved to reservations in Oklahoma or tamed by that time, but settlers did not flock in right away. Breckenridge became a trading post for white buffalo hunters in the 1870s. There was some coal mining along Hubbard Creek in the late 1870s and early 1880s.

Ranching was the chief occupation and Breckenridge was a very small town until the oil boom that started at Ranger spread here in 1918. The population of Breckenridge jumped from a few hundred to about 30,000 by 1921. The population declined rapidly as the boom faded. It is now about 7,000. This is well over half the population of the county. The other town here is Caddo, on US 180 in eastern Stephens County. Caddo grew up around a store N. J. Butler established in the late 1870s. The town supposedly occupies an old Caddo Indian campsite.

Oil and gas production in Stephens County still is very substantial. There is some manufacturing. About 90 percent of the agricultural income comes from livestock.

69

69) The previous courthouse was torn down when the present building was built. The county preserved the entrance as a memorial to earlier county officials — and taxpayers. The previous building had been built in 1883 of red sandstone.

Palo Pinto County

This was an Indian hunting ground into the 1870s but settlers started moving to what is now Palo Pinto County about 1854. George Bevers settled that year near the present town of Graford. Reuben Vaughn moved in the same year.

Several of the big names in the history of the cattle business are associated with this county. Pioneer rancher Oliver Loving brought his herds here in 1855. Loving's partner, Charles Goodnight, moved in the following year. Loving and a partner named John Durkee were the first cowmen to drive a herd of Texas cows directly to a northern market. They delivered a herd to Chicago in 1858.

Cattle raised here by Loving and Goodnight made the first trip to New Mexico by the route that became known as the Goodnight-Loving Trail. This happened shortly after the Civil War. George Webb Slaughter was driving cattle from his spread in Palo Pinto County to Louisiana about the same time. Slaughter had the help of several sons. Three of them later made names for themselves in the cattle business. John B. Slaughter and Will B. Slaughter developed a ranch in Crosby County. Christopher Columbus Slaughter's Long S Ranch eventually spread over several counties in far West Texas.

Goodnight and Loving and a few others were ranching in the area before the legislature created this county from parts of Bosque and Navarro counties in 1856. The county took its name from Palo Pinto Creek. Palo Pinto translates to "spotted stick" in English and it supposedly comes from a variety of oak common here, with a spotted or mottled trunk. The legislature decreed that a town should be established in the center of the county to be the county seat and that the town should be named Golconda. The town was established, but the settlers soon changed the name to Palo Pinto. The county seat never grew very much. Three or four other towns are larger, but Palo Pinto is still the seat of the county government.

The biggest town in the county is Mineral Wells. Settlement began at Mineral Wells in the 1870s. Mineral water believed to have medicinal qualities

70) The oldest public building in Palo Pinto County is the former county jail at Elm and 5th Avenue in Palo Pinto. It now houses the Palo Pinto County Pioneer Museum. Open on summer weekends and by appointment. Free.

70

71

71) *Fancier resorts and newer health fads have done in all the old Texas spas. Mineral Wells was the greatest of them, its popularity peaking in the 1920s.*

New uses have yet to be found for some of the buldings put up in the days when large numbers of people came here to drink and bathe away their aches and pains.

72

72) *Some older Texans still remember attending conventions at the Baker Hotel in Mineral Wells. This was the premier hotel and it drew a lot of trade from Dallas and Fort Worth. The Baker has changed hands several times and various ideas have been put forward concerning it, but it has been a long time since anything happened at the Baker.*

73) *Most of the old base that was known at various times as Camp Wolters, Wolters Air Force Base, and Fort Wolters is actually in Parker County, but the main entrance is just east of Mineral Wells in Palo Pinto County. Weatherford College is using some of the buildings. Part of the base is an industrial park.*

73

was discovered in 1881, and the town site was laid out. The town's first boom began after 1885 when the Crazy Well was completed. Word went around that water from this well could cure hysteria and produce assorted other benefits for people drinking it and bathing in it. Crazy Water was bottled and shipped all over. Thousands of people came to Mineral Wells to drink and bathe in the mineral waters. A resort hotel called Hexagon House was built in 1897. Several other hotels followed. Four hundred wells were producing mineral waters by the 1920s. Mineral Wells was a popular convention center and tourist resort up until World War II.

153

74

74) The access is from Stephens County but the Possum Kingdom State Park is in Palo Pinto County, as most of Possum Kingdom Lake is. The park was not started until after 1952 but the lake was completed in 1941 as the first project of the agency that became the Brazos River Authority. Part of the money came from the WPA and there is a story that President Franklin Roosevelt personally chose the name. Camping. Fee.

The establishment of an army base brought a new boom to Mineral Wells in 1940. The population of the city jumped from about 6,000 to 11,000 during the war years. Camp Wolters actually started as a summer training camp for the 56th Brigade of the Texas National Guard in 1925. It was named for brigade commander Jacob F. Wolters. The army took the base over and expanded it in 1940 into a training center for infantry replacements. The Air Force used the base for a while in the 1950s and changed the name to Wolters Air Force Base. The army returned in 1956 and turned Wolters into a school for helicopter pilots. Thousands of pilots trained here for the war in Vietnam.

I-20 cuts across the southern edge of Palo Pinto County, missing Mineral Wells and Palo Pinto. The Interstate passes close by the old coal mining towns of Mingus and Strawn. Palo Pinto County produces some oil and gas and sends several million dollars' worth of cattle and hogs to market every year.

Parker County

Part of what is now Parker County was included in a colonial grant the Mexican government awarded to Stephen F. Austin in the 1830s. But there were no attempts at settlement here until 1849. Rancher Dan Waggoner moved here in 1855. Rancher and trail driver Oliver Loving established his home here the same year. Loving grazed his cows here and in what is now Palo Pinto County.

Parker County was a little better protected than some other West Texas counties in the frontier days, because of its location between Fort Worth and Fort Belknap. But Indian attacks were not uncommon during the first years after settlement started in 1849.

The legislature created this county in 1855 from parts of Bosque and Navarro counties. The county and the county seat were named for people present when

154

75

76

77

78

75) *Each year in April, car clubs from all over put on a big swap meeting at the Pate Museum of Transportation. A pasture outside the museum is crowded with vehicles and parts for sale or trade at the annual Pate Swap Meet. It is one of the biggest such events in the country.*

A collection of classic and vintage cars assembled by the late A. M. Pate, Jr. of Fort Worth is on display at the Pate Museum outside Cresson in the southeast corner of Parker County. Open daily except Monday, 9 am to 5 pm. Free.

76) *The elegant Parker County courthouse in Weatherford is carefully maintained. It was built of limestone in 1886.*

77) *Parker County was named for Isaac Parker of the clan that established Fort Parker in 1834 in what is now Limestone County. Isaac Parker was a member of the legislature when Parker County was created. He was living near Weatherford when he died in 1883.*

78) *The old Santa Fe passenger depot in Weatherford survives as a Visitor Center and Chamber of Commerce office with some railroad relics outside.*

155

79

79) Two early log cabins have been combined to make a small museum in Holland Lake Park in Weatherford. One of these cabins is said to have been the Dan Waggoner Ranch headquarters in 1885.

80) The late Mary Martin lived in Weatherford when she was a girl. Mary's son, Larry Hagman, lived in Weatherford when he was a teenager and finished high school here.

No monuments to the villianous star of Dallas have been erected in Weatherford, yet, but there is a statue of his mother. It depicts Mary in her role as Peter Pan and it stands on the grounds of the Weatherford Library, at 1214 Charles Street.

80

156

81) The First United Methodist Church of Weatherford was built in 1893 at South Main and East Columbia.

81

this took place. The county was named for Isaac Parker. He was representing Tarrant County in the Texas House of Representatives at the time. Parker was a member of the pioneer clan that established Fort Parker in what is now Limestone County in 1834. He was an uncle of the famous Comanche captive, Cynthia Ann Parker.

The Parker County seat was named for Jefferson Weatherford. He was representing Dallas County in the Texas Senate when this county and county seat were created.

Springtown was established in 1857 and called Littletonville until the 1870s when the name was changed to Springtown. Azle was established in the 1860s and called Fowler's Store and then O'Bar before it was named Azle in 1881 for Dr. Azle Stewart. A substantial part of Azle is in Tarrant County. Reno was founded in 1860. Aledo developed in 1879 when the Texas and Pacific Railroad came through. Bennett was named for George Bennett when he established the Acme Brick Company there in 1891. Acme was the first plant

82) *The highest ground in Weatherford is occupied by the house banker C. D. Harnett built for his family in 1897. It was called "Denver" because it was the coolest spot in town.*

82

83

83) *The Texas Grand Lodge of the Knights of Pythias built this home outside Weatherford in 1909 for widows and orphans. The Knights of Pythias once had 30,000 members in Texas.*

in Texas to produce high-grade pressed brick. The company has become one of the biggest producers of face brick in the United States.

There are several popular resorts around the three lakes in this county. Lake Weatherford, east of the county seat, is on the Clear Fork of the Trinity. Lake Mineral Wells is on the western edge of the county. The northern end of Lake Granbury, on the Brazos, is in the southern end of Parker County. The western suburbs of Fort Worth reach into eastern Parker County and this kind of development is sure to continue, along I-20.

Parker County's fame as a producer of watermelons dates from 1904. Four big melons from this county won a gold medal at the World's Fair in St. Louis that year. This encouraged people to ask for watermelons grown in Parker County. It also encouraged farmers in Parker County to grow more watermelons. Peaches, peanuts, and watermelons are still important to the economy here, but the biggest part of the agricultural income is from livestock. There are some modest oil and gas fields, too.

Park

Lake Mineral Wells State Park, off US 180, 4 miles east of Mineral Wells. Camping. Fee.

84

84) J. Brown builds replica stagecoaches in a shop behind his home in Weatherford. His customers include the Disney parks and the Texas Parks and Wildlife Department. You probably have seen J. Brown stagecoaches in the movies.

The Wichita Falls Area

Wichita, Clay, Archer, Young, Jack, Wise,
Montague, Cooke, and Denton counties.

Some of the major events in the contest between Texans and the Plains Indians occurred in this part of the state. The Brazos and Comanche Indian reservations were here.

One of the major links to the Chisholm Trail crossed the Red River in Montague County and the Butterfield Overland stages rolled through Cooke, Montague, Wise, Jack, and Young counties on their trips between Missouri and California.

161

the Wichita and Taovaya tribes were living in this area when ish explorers came through in the 1780s. There were no settle-nial times. The Kiowa and Comanche Indians had moved in by first settlers ventured this far west.

A riverboat captain named Mabel Gilbert was probably the first permanent white settler. He built a house for his family in 1856 on the Red River at the mouth of a tributary he named Gilbert Creek. Indian raids forced the Gilberts to move east to Montague County in 1857, and again in 1862, but they returned both times.

There were very few settlers here when the legislature created the county in 1858 from part of the Young Territory. The new county was named for the Wichita River, which had been named for the Indians. There were not enough people to justify a county government until years later. And there always was some doubt whether all the 150 signers of the petition for organization actually were living in the county when the petition was filed in 1882. But the county was organized that year and the voters chose Wichita Falls to be the county seat.

Wichita Falls was founded in 1876 by the heirs of J. A. Scott of Mississippi. Scott reputedly had won the scrip for the land in a poker game sometime before he died. The town was named for a little waterfall on the Wichita River that later was destroyed by floods. Fewer than a dozen families were living in Wichita Falls when the town was designated the county seat. But Wichita Falls began growing almost as soon as it became the county seat because the Fort Worth and Denver Railroad laid its tracks through the town site the same year. Wichita Falls became a major shipping point and supply center for the ranches south of the Red River.

2

1, previous page) The Wichita Falls Museum and Art Center has a collection representative of most of the major themes in American art. Monday through Saturday, 9 am to 4:30 pm, Sunday 1 pm to 5 pm. Free.

2) The little waterfall on the Wichita River that gave Wichita Falls its name disappeared a long time ago. It's been replaced by a more impressive waterfall the city has created in a park just off US 287 near downtown.

3

3) *Wichita Falls banker Frank Kell built this house at 900 Bluff Street in 1909. The Wichita County Heritage Society maintains it as a house museum, with the original Kell furnishings. Open Sundays 2 pm to 4 pm.*

4

4) *Con men of all degrees swarmed into Wichita County during the oil boom of the nineteen-teens. Evidence of one of their schemes still stands in an alley off Seventh Street in Wichita Falls. The promoters claimed they were building a major office building when they sold shares to North- erners. What they built was a four-story building, ten feet by sixteen feet, too small for any purpose except to make a profit for the promoters. It's been known since 1919 as "The Littlest Sky- scraper."*

163

5

5) *Sheppard Air Force Base was established north of Wichita Falls in 1941. It was closed at the end of World War II, then reactivated in 1948. It was named for the late United States Senator Morris Sheppard.*

6

6) *Nothing remains of the training base the Aviation Section of the Army Signal Corps had outside Wichita Falls during World War I.*

The population of Wichita Falls and Wichita County increased more dramatically after oil was discovered at Electra and Burkburnett.

The Electra town site was originally part of the huge Waggoner Ranch founded by Dan Waggoner and his son, W. T. Waggoner, when they moved their operations from Wise and Clay counties in 1878. The settlement that became Electra was first called Beaver, for Beaver Creek. The name was changed to Waggoner, and then to Electra, to honor W. T. Waggoner's granddaughter.

The Waggoners sold the town site and 91,000 acres to the north of it to real estate developers in 1905. The developers brought in prospective buyers by the trainload. They sold a lot of land and buyers here had more reason to be pleased than did buyers dealing with some other Texas land promoters.

Some of the buyers got rich after the Electra Oil Field discovery well blew in on April Fool's Day, 1911. The Waggoners got richer than anybody else because they still had more land than they had sold. They went into the oil business all the way. The Waggoners for a time had their own refinery and a chain of service stations selling gasoline that carried the same three D brand the Waggoner cows and horses wore.

The settlement that became Burkburnett was originally called Nesterville. It apparently was given that name by the cowhands on the 6666 Ranch. Cowmen referred to people trying to settle on rangeland in the cow country as nesters. It was not a term of endearment. The 6666 Ranch today is near Guthrie in King County, but Samuel Burk Burnett started here. The name of the town was changed to Gilbert, to honor the first settler, but the name was changed again when the town moved in 1907 to get on the new Wichita Falls and Northwestern rail line. Theodore Roosevelt is said to have suggested the name Burkburnett.

Burkburnett became famous in 1918 when completion of the Fowler Well Number One proved that an oil field actually discovered in 1912 was a substantial one. Fifty-six rigs were drilling within the town site a short time later. The Burkburnett Field produced 40,000,000 barrels of oil in less than

7

7) *Burkburnett was the scene of one of the classic Texas oil booms. Two hundred wells were drilled within the town in the first three months after the discovery well came in, in 1918. The 1941 movie "Boomtown" was based on a story set in Burkburnet.*

165

two years, but production declined after a few fat years. Burkburnett never ranked as a really major field. But the boom was the kind you read about. Burkburnett was the inspiration for Rex Beach's novel *Flowing Gold*.

Iowa Park developed on the Fort Worth and Denver line in the 1880s. It was called Daggett's Switch originally. The name was changed because a number of the early settlers came from Iowa.

Many Texas counties produce more oil and gas than Wichita County produces now. But the oil and gas income still is several times what the county's farms and ranches earn. The county also has a number of industrial and manufacturing plants and a major air base.

One of the major army air training bases during World War I was located five miles south of Wichita Falls. Call Field was named for Lieutenant Loren Call, and 500 army flyers were commissioned there before the base was closed in 1919.

Clay County

This county may have been named for Senator Henry Clay of Kentucky. Or it may have been named for the type of soil that is common here. The legislature did not spell out the reason for the name when the county was created from part of Cooke County in 1857.

There certainly were reasons why Texas lawmakers might have wanted to honor Henry Clay. He had been secretary of state; he had been a candidate for president; and he was the chief architect of the Compromise of 1850. The compromise was one of the efforts made to prevent the dispute over slavery from destroying the Union. Texas collected ten million dollars from the Federal

8) *This marker near Petrolia in northeast Clay County commemorates two historic events: The discovery of the Petrolia Oil and Gas Field in 1907 and the first oil well in North Texas, brought in accidentally by a farmer drilling for water, in 1901.*

8

9

9) *Henrietta has been the county seat of Clay County since 1874. The present courthouse was built in 1884.*

10

10) Lake Arrowhead on the Little Wichita River furnishes water for the city of Wichita Falls. Lake Arrowhead State Park is on the west bank of this lake, off FM 1954. Camping. Fee.

Government in return for giving up her claims to parts of New Mexico, Oklahoma, Colorado, and Wyoming, as part of the compromise.

Some accounts have claimed that the county seat of Clay County was named for Henry Clay's wife. But Mrs. Clay's name was Lucretia and the Clay County seat is named Henrietta. The town may have been named for Clay himself. Somebody may have thought a feminine version of his first name was more suitable for a town.

There were Spanish expeditions in this area in 1759, 1786, and 1787. There were no Spanish settlements. The Taovaya Indians were here in Spanish times, but the Comanches controlled the area by the 1800s. The early settlers were ranchers. There were small settlements at Cambridge and Henrietta by 1860. The population had just surpassed one hundred when the Civil War began. A few ranchers hung on during the war, but most of the settlers moved

11

11) The army once considered this spot in southeast Clay County as a site for the frontier fort that eventually was built in what is now Jack County. There wasn't enough water for a fort but Buffalo Springs provided water for generations of Indians and a number of white buffalo hunters. The marker is at the intersection of FM 174 and FM 3077.

away and the county government was abandoned because of Indian attacks. The county government was not reorganized until 1873. The original county seat was Cambridge, but Cambridge died when the Fort Worth and Denver Railroad laid its line through Henrietta. The county government and most of the population of Cambridge had moved to Henrietta by 1882.

Byers was established on the Wichita Valley Railroad line in 1904 by George and A. W. Byers. The first oil was discovered in Clay County in 1901, accidentally. The discoverer was trying to drill a water well. This happened in the northern part of the county near a settlement that was promptly named Oil City. The oil production reached serious proportions in 1904 with the development of the Petrolia field and the name of Oil City was changed to Petrolia. The Petrolia field has always produced more gas than oil. Natural gas was being piped from this field to Dallas and Fort Worth by 1913. There is substantial oil and gas production still. Farms in Clay County produce some wheat, cotton, and sorghum, but most of the agricultural income is from cattle and hogs. County population is around 10,000 with about one third of it concentrated in Henrietta.

Archer County

The activities of the Kiowa and Comanche Indians kept settlers out of this part of Texas until the late 1850s. There is no record of any white settlers at all being in this area in 1858, when the legislature separated it from the Fannin District, made it a county, and named it for Branch T. Archer. The legislature decreed at the same time that the county seat would be a town named Archer City.

Dr. Branch T. Archer had come to Texas from Virginia sometime before 1832. He settled in Brazoria County and he was soon taking an active part in revolutionary politics. Archer was president of the Consultation of 1835 when that body decided Texas should fight to become a separate state in the

12

12) *Descendants of some of the original German settlers of Windthorst still live here and still attend sevices at St. Mary's Church. Windthorst is at the eastern edge of Archer County.*

13

13) *One of the markers on the courthouse grounds in Archer City notes that this is one of the places where the notorious badman Jesse James sometimes hid out, in the 1870s. He had a sister living in Archer County. Archer City has been the county seat since Archer County was created in 1858. The present courthouse was built in 1910.*

Mexican Republic. He was in the United States as one of the commissioners enlisting recruits and political support when the Convention of 1836 resolved that Texas' objective was independence from Mexico. Archer was a member of the first congress of the Republic of Texas.

The Texas Rangers Frontier Regiment had an outpost here in Archer County during the Civil War. It was in the southern end of the county where the road to Fort Belknap crossed the West Fork of the Trinity. A few ranchers moved into the county after the end of the war. The first permanent settlement was established in 1874.

Texas Rangers discovered nodules of copper on the surface of the ground here in the 1860s. Mining companies tried in 1880 and again in 1899 to

169

15

14

14) Archer County was named for Dr. Branch T. Archer, one of the early advocates of Texas independence and a member of the first congress of the Republic of Texas.

15) The Archer County Historical Museum occupies the old jail building the county built in 1910, a block off the courthouse square. Exhibits include the original Archer County gallows. Open Saturdays 9 am to 6 pm and Sundays 1 pm to 6 pm. Free.

16) The movie version of "The Last Picture Show" was filmed in Claude, but this is probably the movie house author Larry McMurtry had in mind when he wrote the novel in 1966. The Royal was the only theater in Archer City when McMurtry was growing up here. The last picture showed here a long time ago.

16

exploit the resource, but no major underground deposit ever was found. The first railroad reached Archer County in 1890. The oil was discovered in 1920.

Holliday, in northern Archer County, was founded in 1889 and named for a creek that had been named for John Holliday. Windthorst, east of Archer City was named for Ludwig Windthorst. It was founded by F. T. Ledergerber and Thomas Law in 1891 and settled by German Catholics.

17

17) The Navy sends up radio signals from this lengthy antenna in southern Archer County to keep track of objects orbiting in space.

Boating and fishing have become very popular in the ranch country since so many dams have been built. There are several campgrounds and resorts around Lake Kickapoo, on the North Fork of the Little Wichita River, 12 miles northwest of Archer City. A small part of Diversion Lake is in the northwest corner of Archer County. Part of Lake Wichita is in the northeast corner, and the upper end of Lake Arrowhead reaches into the eastern edge of Archer County.

Most of the land here is in ranches and most of the agricultural income is from livestock. There are several dozen dairy farms in the county. The oil and gas fields bring in much more money than the farms and ranches. Population of the county is only about 8,000.

Young County

The Spanish probably first became aware of the area that is now Young County in 1759, when Diego Ortiz Parilla came through on his way to the Red River to make war on the Taovaya Indians. There were no settlements. The area was occupied only by Indians until 1851. The U.S. Army established an outpost that year to protect settlers and the road to California. The post was named for Mexican War veteran William G. Belknap of New York. General Belknap died at the post very shortly after it was established.

Fort Belknap was a station on the Butterfield Overland Mail Line. A stage and mail line from Dallas and Fort Worth connected with the Butterfield line at the fort. The earliest settlers in the area were mostly people doing business with the fort. Elijah Skidmore may have been the first white person to try to settle here. He established a homestead near the present city of Graham in 1851 but he was killed by Indians a few months later.

The presence of the troops at Fort Belknap was one of the factors that encouraged state and federal authorities to establish an Indian reservation here

18

18) Fort Belknap was established before the legislature created Young County. The little settlement at the fort was the original county seat. This was the largest fort on the Texas frontier before the Civil War.

19

20

19) Some relics of frontier days have been preserved in one of the old buildings. What is left of Fort Belknap is now a county park. The presence of this fort influenced the decision to establish an Indian reservation nearby.

20) Robert Neighbors was the Texas Indian Superintendent during the reservation experiment. Many whites thought he was far too sympathetic toward the Indians. This marker at Fort Belknap doesn't mention it, but Major Belknap was shot to death — and not by an Indian.

172

in 1855. The reservation was established on the Brazos here at the same time the Comanche Reservation was established next door in Throckmorton County. Both reservations were under the supervision of Robert S. Neighbors. The reservation here was called the Brazos Reservation. Small bands of Caddo, Anadarko, Waco, and Tonkawa Indians started farms on the reservation. Some of the Indian braves served as scouts for the troops stationed at Fort Belknap. But there were strong feelings against the Indians among some of the settlers.

A former Indian agent named John R. Baylor put considerable energy into fomenting distrust and suspicion of the Indians. Robert Neighbors had fired Baylor from his agency job because he thought Baylor was prejudiced against Indians. Baylor had no reason to want Neighbors or the reservations to succeed.

Baylor led a foray onto the Brazos Reservation in May of 1859 that led to the fight that caused the reservations here and in Throckmorton County to be closed. Agent Neighbors personally escorted the Indians across the Red River into Oklahoma. He wrote his wife then that they had left the land of the Philistines. Neighbors was said to be the white man with the most influence among Texas Indians at that time. Many whites thought there must be something wrong with a white man who was that concerned about Indians. Neighbors was shot in the back by a man he had never met shortly after he returned from Oklahoma. He died in the street in the little settlement outside Fort Belknap. Twelve years later, Fort Belknap and Camp Cooper were major supply bases for Ranald Mackenzie's campaign to exterminate the Comanches.

21

21) Young County was reorganized after the Civil War and the county seat was moved to Graham where it has been ever since. The present courthouse was built in Graham in 1931.

22

22) A driller hoping for an oil well tapped into a reservoir of hot mineral water outside of South Bend in 1929. People have been coming to the well ever since to bathe in the hot smelly water that still pours from it. South Bend is in the south end of Young County.

The incident that provoked the Mackenzie campaign occurred here in Young County in May of 1871. A wagon train owned by government contractor Henry Warren was hauling a supply of corn for the horses and mules at Fort Griffin in Shackelford County. A band of Comanche and Kiowa Indians surprised the wagon train near the present town of Graham. The Indians killed seven teamsters and mutilated some of them. One of the survivors walked to Fort Richardson in the next county to report the attack.

General William T. Sherman was making a tour of the frontier at the time to find out for himself whether the Indian problem was as bad as he had been told it was. Sherman was at Fort Richardson when the survivor of the wagon train raid arrived there. Sherman ordered Colonel Mackenzie to pursue the Indians, and the pursuit became a crusade after Sherman reached Fort Sill and found out that the raid had been executed by Indians illegally absent from the Oklahoma reservations.

The legislature created Young County in 1856 from parts of Fannin and Bosque counties. The settlement at Fort Belknap was designated the county seat. There were almost six hundred people in the county when the Civil War began. U.S. troops left Fort Belknap and all the other Texas forts then. Indian raids increased. Many settlers moved east to safer areas. The population in this county was down to fewer than 200 by the time the Civil War ended. The county was reorganized in 1874 and the county seat was moved to Graham. Gus and Edwin Graham had established this town in 1872. The Graham brothers had a salt business here.

Graham is the biggest town in Young County. Olney is the next biggest. It was established in the 1880s and probably was named for Richard Olney.

23) James Donnell built this mill on the Clear Fork of the Brazos at Eliasville in 1876. Eliasville is in the southwest corner of Young County.

23

Newcastle started as a coal mining camp in the 1880s and was named for the English mining town.

Lake Graham on Salt Creek was completed by the city of Graham in 1958. The upper end of the Possum Kingdom Reservoir reaches into the southeastern corner of Young County. The Brazos River Authority created Possum Kingdom Lake by building the Morris Sheppard Dam in Palo Pinto County in 1941.

The first railroad reached Graham in 1902. Oil was discovered in 1917. The oil and gas fields produce far more income today than the farms and ranches in Young County.

Jack County

The Indian inhabitants of this part of Texas were not disturbed until 1854. B. L. Ham settled that year at a place that was later named Bryson for property owner Henry Bryson. Several people settled the same year around a salt deposit and named their community Salt Hill. Settlement began on Lost Creek in 1855. The settlers called their settlement Lost Creek for a time and then changed the name to Mesquiteville. The name was changed again to Jacksborough in 1858 when the residents of the county voted to make the settlement the county seat. The name was shortened to Jacksboro in 1899.

This county and the county seat were named for a couple of early Texas settlers. Patrick C. and William H. Jack were brothers and both were lawyers. They came to Texas in 1830. Patrick Jack was arrested with William Barret Travis during a dispute between colonists and Mexican authorities at Anahuac in 1832. William Jack fought at San Jacinto. Both men died in 1844. The legislature named this county for them when it was created from part of Cooke County in 1856.

A newspaper published in Jacksboro between 1858 and 1860 helped generate the sentiment that forced removal of the Indian reservations from Young and

175

Throckmorton counties. The paper was called *The Whiteman*. It was devoted to attacks upon Indians, Indian agents, and Sam Houston.

The Butterfield Road came through Jacksboro and the army decided to build a fort here after the end of the Civil War. The area had been considered reasonably safe before the war. There were more than 1,600 people living in Jack County in 1860. But Indian raids increased while most of the men were away at war, and the population was under 700 when the war ended.

People started moving back to Jacksboro and Jack County after Fort Richardson was built in 1867. The fort was established on Lost Creek just south of Jacksboro by units of the U.S. Sixth Cavalry. The fort was named for Civil War (Union) hero Israel Richardson.

Colonel Ranald Mackenzie was in command at Fort Richardson when General William T. Sherman came through on tour of inspection in 1871. It was while he was at Fort Richardson that Sherman learned the Kiowas and Comanches had killed seven teamsters in an attack on Henry Warren's wagon train in adjacent Young County. Sherman went on to Fort Sill after telling Mackenzie to find the Indians and punish them. Mackenzie never caught up with the raiders. They beat it back across the Red River to the Oklahoma reservations where they were supposed to be living. But Indian Agent Laurie Tatum got Kiowa Chief Satanta to admit that he and Chief Satank and Chief Big Tree had led the raid in Young County. Tatum turned the three chiefs over to Sherman. The general ordered them taken back to Jack County to stand trial.

24

24) Several Texas counties demolished old courthouses and put up new ones during the New Deal days in the late 1930s. Some of the old courthouses didn't particularly need to be replaced, but new courthouses meant jobs and the federal government's WPA program was a considerable incentive. The courthouse in Jacksboro is a typical WPA court building. It was completed in 1939.

25) The courthouse contrasts with the 19th Century stone buldings surrounding the courthouse square. Settlement began here in 1855. Jacksboro has been the county seat since 1858.

25

26

26) The victors of the Civil War were running the country in 1871. U. S. Grant was president. William T. Sherman was General of the Army. Sherman had doubts about the stories he heard from Texas about the hostility of the Plains Indians. He came to find out for himself and what he found out, here in Jack County, brought on the campaign that ended the Indians' control of the Texas High Plains.

Chief Satank was shot to death when he tried to escape. But Satanta and Big Tree were charged with murder and put on trial in District Court in Jacksboro on July 5, 1871. It was the first time Indians ever had been tried in a white man's court. The prosecutor was a young lawyer named Samuel W. T. Lanham. He later was elected governor, and he was the father of the late congressman Fritz Lanham. Satanta and Big Tree were convicted of murder and sentenced to death. Federal authorities persuaded Reconstruction Governor E. J. Davis to commute the sentences and later persuaded him to parole the two chiefs.

General Sherman was outraged. He wrote Governor Davis a letter predicting that Satanta and Big Tree would soon be scalping people again and suggesting that it might be appropriate if they took Davis' scalp first. Chief Big Tree settled down and became a deacon in the Baptist church. But Sherman's prediction was right in Satanta's case. Satanta was arrested again and returned to the Huntsville penitentiary where he committed suicide in 1878.

27

27) *General Sherman was staying at Fort Richardson when he learned Indians had massacred seven teamsters working for a government contractor. And it had happened in an area the general had passed through only a day earlier. The old fort is now Fort Richardson State Park. The military hospital has been rebuilt. There is a museum inside.*

The park entrance is off US 281 just south of Jacksboro. Camping. Fee.

The campaign Sherman and Mackenzie started against the Comanches here in 1871 ended in 1874 when Mackenzie scattered the last band of Comanches in the Panhandle. The army abandoned Fort Richardson in 1878. The frontier had shifted westward. The troops moved from Fort Richardson to Fort Griffin in Shackelford County and then closed Fort Griffin in 1881.

Jacksboro is the biggest town in Jack County. Bryson is the second biggest. Antelope was established in the 1850s and named for a Kiowa campground known as Antelope Springs. The pioneers named Wizard Wells for the mineral springs thought by the Kiowas to have medicinal value. The Tarrant County Water Control and Improvement District Number 1 built Lake Bridgeport on the West Fork of the Trinity River. The dam is in Wise County. The lake backs up into western Jack County.

The first railroad reached Jacksboro in 1898. There is substantial oil and gas production and some farming in Jack County but most of the land is devoted to ranching.

Wise County

This area was occupied by the Delaware Indians when the first white settler moved in about 1854. The Delawares were Eastern Indians. Some of them moved into Texas in the 1820s. The first white settler probably was Sam Woody of Tennessee. He built a cabin about nine miles southeast of the present city of Decatur in 1854. Other settlers evidently followed pretty close behind Woody. A Methodist congregation was organized at the Sand Hill community near what is now Decatur in 1854.

The legislature took part of Cooke County to create this county in 1856. The county was named for Henry A. Wise. He was governor of Virginia at

28) *The log cabin built by the first white settler in Wise County in 1854 still stands on an unmarked gravel road south of Decatur. The builder was Sam Woody from Tennessee.*

29) *Wise County has one of the more picturesque courthouses in Texas. It was built in Decatur in 1896 and restored in 1989.*

30

30) *Dan Waggoner made the first real money he ever made in the cattle business while he was living in Wise County. He built this home in Decatur in 1883. The Waggoner Ranch moved farther west a few years later.*

the time, but he had been a member of the U.S. Senate in the 1840s, where he was a proponent of the annexation of Texas.

The town designated to be the county seat was originally called Bishop's Hill because it was founded by a man named Absolom Bishop. The name was changed later to Taylorsville in honor of President Zachary Taylor. It was renamed Decatur in 1857. The present name honors the memory of Commodore Stephen Decatur of the U.S. Navy. He was a hero of the War of 1812 and the campaign against the Barbary pirates. But Decatur is best remembered for a toast he proposed once at a dinner in his honor: "Our contry: In her intercourse with foreign nations, may she always be right; but our country, right or wrong!" Patriots and politicians have been quoting Decatur ever since.

The Butterfield mail line began running through Wise County in 1858. The settlement that became the town of Bridgeport developed at a toll bridge built by some local speculators in 1860 at the Butterfield Road crossing of the West Fork of the Trinity River.

There was considerable sentiment in North Texas in favor of the Union during the Civil War. Union supporters here had a secret society. One of the Unionists drank too much one night and tried to recruit the wrong man. The Unionist group was exposed. Five of the Unionists were tried and convicted of treason and hanged in Decatur.

Dan Waggoner of Tennessee brought a small herd of longhorns here from Hopkins County in the early 1850s. Waggoner and his son, W. T. Waggoner, drove their first herd of cattle from Wise County to market in Kansas in 1870. That trip turned the profit that started the Waggoner Ranch on its way to becoming one of the most successful enterprises in the history of ranching. Decatur was the Waggoner Ranch headquarters.

The names of the county and the county seat were incorporated into the jargon of crapshooters a long time ago. Players trying to coax the dice into coming up on eight have been chanting, "Eighter from Decatur, the county seat of Wise" for generations.

One of the big-time badmen of the gangster era put Wise County in the headlines in 1933. George Kelley and his gang kidnapped Oklahoma oilman Charles Urschel and held him prisoner on a farm near Paradise until the Urschel family paid $200,000 ransom. The tabloids of the day always referred to Kelley as Machine Gun Kelley. His wife's family owned the farm where Urschel was held. Urschel made it a point to remember what time airplanes flew over the farm each day and that information helped the F.B.I. locate the farm after Urschel was freed, and make the connection between it and Kelley. Machine Gun Kelley was tracked down and sent to Leavenworth where he died in 1954. He is reputed to have been the first person to refer to agents of the Federal Bureau of Investigation as "G-Men."

Coal deposits discovered nearby in the 1870s, and the dam that created Lake Bridgeport have fostered Bridgeport's growth, and it is about the same size as Decatur. The other towns in Wise County are much smaller. Alvord was named for Fort Worth and Denver Railroad President J. B. Alvord. Boyd

31

31) The building housing the Wise County Heritage Museum was once the administration building of the Decatur Baptist College, built in 1893. Monday through Saturday, 9 am to 4:30 pm and Sunday 1 pm to 4:30 pm. Fee.

32

was named for Rock Island Railroad official H. S. Boyd. Chico was founded in 1874 by J. T. Brown and named for his previous hometown in California.

Oil was discovered in Wise County in 1942 and it ranks about even with farming and ranching in the economy here. This is one of the state's most important dairying centers.

Montague County

The Taovaya Indians had a large village on the south side of the Red River in what is now Montague County in the 1700s. The south bank of the river was part of Spanish Texas. The French claimed the north bank as part of Louisiana. The Taovayas were a branch of the Wichita tribe and they were traders. They carried on trade with the French and with the Comanche Indians.

The Spanish decided that somebody had to suffer for it after the Comanches destroyed their San Saba Mission near Menard in 1758. Nobody knew where to find the Comanches because they were nomads. But the Spanish knew they did business with the Taovaya village on the Red River.

Diego Ortiz Parilla came north in 1759 with 500 Spanish and Mexican soldiers to attack the village. It was a mistake. The village was protected by a stockade. The Taovayas and Comanches defending it had French firearms and they outnumbered the attackers. Parilla survived, but he lost the battle.

The Taovayas were gone by the time the first Anglos came to this area. The Anglos discovered a few artifacts that indicated to them that once there had been a fort here. It had been Spanish territory, they knew, so they assumed it was a Spanish fort and that was the name they gave the place. The Comanches were still around so there was very little settlement in the area until after the

33) *The Justin Boot Company started in Montague County and later moved to Fort Worth. Edith Justin didn't want to move to Fort Worth, so she stayed in Nocona, started the Nocona Boot Company and ran it personally for many years.*

33

34

35

34) *A highway department marker near Ringgold testifies that the contractor unknowingly used some sand mixed with gold dust in paving US 81 and US 287 here.*

35) *Saint Jo was first called Head of Elm. It was a regular campsite for early travelers because of the spring that formed the headwaters of Elm Creek.*

Civil War. There was a lot of activity here in the 1870s. One of the cattle trails feeding into the Chisholm Trail crossed the river at Red River Station near the old Taovaya village. The settlement at Spanish Fort was being called Burlington then. It was the last place the trail drivers and their hands could buy supplies before they crossed into Indian Territory.

36 37

36) The first permanent building in the town that became Saint Jo was this saloon. It became an office building and then a bank after Prohibition made saloons illegal. The old saloon building is now a museum. Open daily 8 am to 6 pm. Free.

37) Three other towns are bigger, but Montague has been the county seat since Montague County was organized in 1858. The present courthouse was built in 1913.

H. J. Justin was one of the tradesmen catering to the cattle drivers. Cowmen going north with their herds left orders with Justin's Cowboy Boot Company and then picked up their new boots on the way back south. Justin moved his business to Nocona and changed the name to Justin Boot Company in the middle 1880s, after the railroads came and the trail drives slacked off. The settlement at the old Indian village changed its name from Burlington back to Spanish Fort.

There was a small settlement at the site before, but it was the arrival of the Gainesville, Henrietta, and Western Railroad in 1887 that made Nocona a town. The settlement was named for Peta Nocona. He was the Comanche husband of the kidnapped Cynthia Ann Parker and the father of Comanche chief Quanah Parker.

The place most frequented by Anglos in the earliest days here was a spring at the head of the Elm Fork of the Trinity River near the eastern border of what is now Montague County. Captain Randolph Marcy and his men camped here when they were blazing the trail for the California immigrants in 1849. Units of the Second U.S. Cavalry, coming in from Missouri to man the forts on the Texas frontier, camped here in 1855. A few people started settling around the spring and they called their settlement Head of Elm. I. H. Boggers and Joe Howells bought some land at Head of Elm in 1873 and laid out a town site. They named their town Joe, for Joe Howells. Boggers and others started calling it Saint Jo, because Howells drank conspicuously less than the other early settlers. Saint Jo was already on its way to becoming a town when the Gainesville, Henrietta, and Western Railroad came through in 1887.

The first railroad to reach Montague county was the Fort Worth and Denver. This line created the towns of Sunset and Bowie when it laid its tracks across the southwest corner of the county in 1881 and 1882. The town site for Bowie was laid out in August of 1882. The railroad put on a barbecue picnic to help sell lots. Bowie became an important shipping point and it is still the biggest town in the county. Bowie was named for the Alamo hero Jim Bowie.

Montague County was created from part of Cooke County in 1857 and named for the pioneer surveyor and Mexican War hero Daniel Montague. The voters elected, when the county was organized in 1858, to establish a new town in the center of the county to be the county seat. The new town was named for the county. Montague is still the county seat but most of the population is in the railroad towns. Bowie, Nocona, and Saint Jo are all bigger than Montague.

Settlement began at the town that is now Ringgold in 1872. The town site was laid out when the Gainesville, Henrietta, and Western Railroad came through in 1893. Joe Harris had owned the land, so the town was first called Harrisonia, but it was later changed to Ringgold because that was Mrs. Harris' maiden name.

38

38) Sculptor Jack Glover runs the Trading Post and Old West Museum at Sunset. Open daily 8 am to 6 pm. Fee.

The city of Bowie created Lake Amon G. Carter on Big Sandy Creek in 1956. Amon G. Carter lived in Bowie when he was a boy. He went to work for the *Fort Worth Star Telegram* in 1905 and bought the paper in 1908. He put the first Texas television station on the air in 1947 and was the leading citizen of Fort Worth until he died in 1955. The North Montague County Water Supply District created Lake Nocona on Farmer's Creek in 1960.

Oil and gas were discovered in Montague County in 1916. Farming was much more important in the earlier days than it is today. Farms here still produce cotton, peanuts, peaches, and apples. But there is much more ranching than farming.

Cooke County

The Indians had this part of Texas to themselves until 1847 when the Texas Rangers established a little fort about three miles southeast of the present city of Gainesville. This post was named Fort Fitzhugh for the officer in command and it was designated the county seat when the legislature created this county from part of Fannin County in 1848. The settlement at Fort Fitzhugh was called Liberty briefly before it was abandoned when the county government moved to Gainesville in 1850.

The county was named for William G. Cooke. He came to Texas in 1835 to fight in the revolution. He served as quartermaster general of the Republic of Texas and adjutant general of the militia before he died in 1847.

Gainesville was named for General Edmund P. Gaines of the U.S. Army. Gaines was in command of the U.S. troops in Louisiana during the Texas Revolution. He moved some troops into Nacogdoches to keep the peace after the Texans won the Battle of San Jacinto, and he kept them there until the

39) The ground floor of this old building in Leonard Park in Gainesville is reputed to be the original Cooke County Jail.

39

40) *The late famous hunter, animal trainer, and author Frank Buck was born in Gainesville in 1884. Buck produced several movies about his exploits before he died in Houston in 1950.*

40

41) *The zoo in Leonard Park in Gainesville is named for Frank Buck. The park was named for John T. Leonard. He was the founder of the* Gainesville Register *and mayor of Gainesville 1901-1909. Leonard died in 1935 after suffering a heart attack in this park.*

41

government of the Republic of Texas was formally organized. Texans generally assumed Gaines would have helped them fight the Mexicans if it had become necessary.

Gainesville was a regular stop on the original Butterfield Overland Mail Line. Some of the early settlers were dropouts from the California migration.

This part of Texas was very vulnerable to Indian raids during the Civil War when most of the able-bodied men were away. Indians from the Oklahoma Territory continued to harass settlers for several years after the war ended. A band of Kiowas rode into Cooke County in January of 1868 and killed 13 settlers. They kidnapped another ten.

Opinion was pretty evenly divided in this part of Texas on the question of secession in 1861. The people of Texas generally were in favor of secession.

187

42) The old Cloud-Stark House on South Dixon at Church is now an office. There are several other fine old homes along Church Street, nearby.

The vote in the election of February of 1861 was 44,317 in favor of secession and 13,020 against it. But more people voted against secession than voted for it in Cooke County and it was the same in several other counties in this part of Texas.

Some of the opponents of secession formed a secret society to work against the Confederacy and for the Union. They called their society the Peace Party. The party was especially strong in Cooke County. It was exposed when a drunken member tried to enlist a staunch secessionist in the movement. The secessionist joined long enough to find out the identity of the other members.

Several of the supposed members of the Peace Party were lynched in the excitement following the exposure. Confederate troops rounded up more than one hundred other alleged members and they were tried by a "Citizens' Court." The court found 39 men guilty of conspiracy, insurrection, disloyalty, or treason. All 39 were hanged in Gainesville in October of 1862. Surviving Union sympathizers were a good bit more careful after that.

The Little Theater in Gainesville put on a burlesque circus to raise some money in 1930. The show was so successful that it grew into the Gainesville Community Circus. This amateur production was the third biggest circus in the world for several years. But it never recovered from a fire that destroyed most of the circus equipment in 1954.

Muenster is the second biggest town in Cooke County. It was established by German Catholics in 1889. Lindsay was also settled by German Catholics, in 1891. Callisburg was established in 1882 and named for early settler Sam Callis. It was near Callisburg that the first successful oil well in Cooke County was drilled in 1924.

43

43) The Santa Fe passenger depot in Gainesville was built in 1882 and it was the busiest place in town for many years, through World War II when thousands of GIs came through on their way to and from Camp Howze, north of town. The railroad gave the depot to the city in the early 1980s and it has been carefully restored.

44) Two brothers named Ross founded the community of Rosston in the 1870s. The store the Ross brothers built is still in business.

44

Lake Texoma backs up into the northeast corner of Cooke County. Texoma was completed by the Army Engineers in 1944. Moss Lake was completed on Fish Creek, north of Gainesville, by the city of Gainesville in 1966.

Ranching was the chief enterprise here until the 1890s. Cotton became more important for a while then. Farmers here still grow some cotton and peanuts and grains. But many farms have been turned back into pasture and livestock again accounts for most of the agricultural income. There is some manufacturing but the oil and gas revenue is the biggest factor in the economy here.

189

Morton Museum of Cooke County. Old City Hall building, 12 pm to 5 pm.

Denton County_____

The area that is now Denton County was occupied by Indians of the Kickapoo, Caddo, Shawnee, and Delaware tribes in the latter days of the Spanish rule. A few Anglo-American traders began to move into the territory bordering the Red River about 1814. The first congress of the Republic of Texas included this area in the original Red River County when it was established in 1836. Fannin County was separated from Red River County in 1837. This area was included in Fannin County until it was separated in 1846 and established as Denton County.

John B. Denton was a frontier preacher, lawyer, and Indian fighter. His parents had died shortly after he was born in Tennessee in 1806. Denton was adopted and taken to Arkansas by a family named Wells. He was working as an itinerant preacher when he moved to Texas about 1837. He took up law, then, and opened an office in Clarksville in Red River County. Denton also joined the Texas Rangers and advanced to captain in the frontier force commanded by Colonel Edward H. Tarrant. Captain Denton was killed in 1841 in a fight with Indians at Village Creek in what is now Tarrant County. The legislature named this county for him.

Most of the area here was included in the grants the Republic of Texas made to the syndicate known as the Peters Colony in the early 1840s. W. S. Peters and his associates contracted to bring in new settlers from outside

45

45) A museum on the ground floor of the Denton County Courthouse in Denton is open Monday through Thursday, 2 pm to 5 pm. The courthouse is a museum piece itself, built in 1896.

46

46) *The school established in Denton in 1890 as North Texas Normal College is now the University of North Texas. There is a historical museum on the campus, open Monday through Friday from 1 pm to 5 pm.*

47

47) *A museum in the basement of the College of Nutrition, Textiles and Human Development at Texas Woman's University features a collection of the inaugural gowns worn by the first ladies of Texas, and a gown worn by our first woman governor. Monday through Friday, 8 am to 5 pm.*

48) Victortian homes built in the 1890s line West Oak Street near downtown, in Denton.

Texas at the rate of at least 200 a year. Most of the original settlers of Denton County were Peters colonists.

Texas had joined the United States and James Pinckney Henderson had been elected governor by the time Denton County was organized. The settlers named the village they chose as their county seat Pinckneyville, in honor of the new governor. The county government moved two years later to a village called Alton. The government and population of Alton moved to a new location in 1850. The new Alton prospered for a while but the voters of the county decided in 1856 to move the county seat to the center of the county. Three ranchers donated 100 acres for a new town site, and the new town was named Denton.

Denton has become a major education center. North Texas State University and Texas Woman's University both are located here. Texas Woman's University is said to be the biggest women's university in the country.

John Denton was buried near where he was killed, after the Battle of Village Creek in 1841. Pioneer rancher John Chisum had Denton's remains moved in 1861 to a new grave on the Chisum Ranch at Bolivar, in Denton County. Chisum moved his operations farther west after the end of the Civil War. The Pioneer Association of Denton County then had Denton's remains moved again. His grave now is on the courthouse lawn in Denton.

Denton is the biggest city in the county. Lewisville is the second biggest. Lewisville was settled by John and Augustus King in 1844 and named in

1855 for B. W. Lewis. Flower Mound grew up around a Presbyterian church established in the 1850s. Pilot Point was established in 1854 by George Newcomb and named for an early landmark. The towns in southern Denton County are suburbs of Dallas and Fort Worth.

Two of the lakes the U.S. Army Corps of Engineers built to control flooding in the Trinity River watershed are located in this county. There are dozens of public parks and commercial resorts around the shores of Lewisville Lake and Grapevine Reservoir. Lewisville Lake is on the Elm Fork of the Trinity. It was known originally as Garza-Little Elm Reservoir. Grapevine Reservoir is on Denton Creek and mostly in Tarrant County, but the upper end extends into southern Denton County. The city of Dallas draws water from both of these lakes.

Sam Bass worked as a cowhand on the Gregg Ranch in southern Denton County from about 1870 until about 1874. Sam was 19 and an orphan when he came to Texas from Indiana in 1870. He knocked around North Texas and made a little money racing a horse he called the Denton Mare after he left the ranch job. He hired out to help drive a herd of longhorns to Nebraska in 1876 and got in with the wrong crowd on the way. Bass and a gang of other cowboys started hijacking stage coaches and trains in Nebraska and then in Texas. His career was cut short when Texas Rangers got a tip from one of his cronies and ambushed Sam as he was about to hold up a bank in Round Rock. The rangers shot him and Sam Bass died two days later, on July 19, 1878. His name appears on every list of noted Texas outlaws, but Sam never was accused of killing anyone.

Oil was discovered in Denton County in 1937 but production has not been significant. The universities and jobs in adjoining counties produce most of the income. The biggest part of the farm income is from livestock.

49) Pioneer flyer Edna Gardner Whyte is still operating the Aero Valley Airport at Roanoke and still flying, in her 80s.

49

Photo Credits

The photographs for this book were made by Ray Miller and his associates, except as noted below. The first number indicates the page; number in parentheses is the photo number.

Attwater Prairie Chicken National Refuge: 12(17)
Baylor University (Texas Collection): 77(17)
Burkburnett Chamber of Comerce: 165(7)
Brown & Root: 138(48)
Central Texas Area Museum: 115(84)
City of Los Angeles: 106(66)
Edna Gladney Home: 130(32)
Fort Worth Star Telegram: 125(17,18)
Gainesville Chamber of Commerce: 187(40)
General Dynamics Corporation: 131(34)
Houston Chronicle: 104(63)
Houston Public Library: 44(74), 57(94), 69, 72(5), 80(21), 91(40), 96(50), 102(58,59), 141(53), 170(15)
Institute of Texan Cultures: 39(66)
Layland Museum: 132(35)
Price, Mary: 109(71)
Texas A&M University: 50(82)
Texas State Library: 94(44), 98(52), 121(9), 148(64), 155(77), 177(26)

Sources

We are indebted to the staffs of the Texas and Local History Room, Houston Public Library; the Texas State Library in Austin; and the Institute of Texan Cultures in San Antonio for assisting us in our research.

Publications furnishing more details concerning the people, places, and events discussed in this modest volume include:

Baylor at Independence by Murray; *Bosque Primer* by Radde; *Buffalo Book, The* by Dary; *Butterfield Overland Mail* by Conkling and Conkling; *Butterfield Overland Mail* by Wright and Bynum; *Fort Griffin on the Texas Frontier* by Rister; *Fort Richardson, Outpost on the Texas Frontier* by Whisenhunt; *Fort Worth, A Frontier Triumph* by Garrett; *Grand Ol' Erath* by Perry; *Handbook of Texas; History of Limestone County, A* by Steele; *History of the Texas Railroads, A* by Reed; *History of Robertson County* by Baker; *History of Waller County, A; Hood County in Picture and Story; Interwoven* by Matthews; *Lone Star* by Fehrenbach; *Mexia Centennial; National Register of Historic Places in Texas; Old Texas Trails* by Williams; *Papers Concerning Robertson's Colony in Texas* by McLean; *Patchwork of Memories, A* by Caffrey; *Texas Almanac 1990-1991; Texas Almanac, 1857-1873, The* by Moore and Day; *Texas Museum Directory; Texas Outlaw Bill Longley, A Texas Hard-Case* by Bartholomew; *Thirty Years of Army Life on the Border* by Marcy; *Warren Wagon Train Raid, The* by Capps; *Why Stop?; William Bollaert's Texas* by Hollan and Butler.

Index

Bold type denotes photograph.

B

Brazos River lock ruin, 46, **46**
Brazos River Suspension Bridge, Waco, 74, **74**
Brazos Valley Museum of Natural Science, 47, **47**
Breckenridge, 149, **149**, 150, 151
Breckinridge, John C., 150
Bremond, 106
Bremond, Paul, 106
Brenham, 62, 64, 65, 66
Brenham, Richard Fox, 62
Briden Cabin, Rio Vista, 134, **134**
Briden, Henry, 131, 134
Bridgeport, 180, 181
Brookesmith, 87
Brookshire, 59
Brookshire, Nathen, 59
Brown County, 85-88
Brown County Museum, 86, **86**
Brown, Henry S., 85
Browning Plantation, 66, **66**
Browning, Robert and Elizabeth Barrett, 72
Browning, W. W., 66
Brown's Mill, 38
Brownwood, 85, 86, 87
Bryan, 49, 51
Bryan Air Base, 50, 51
Bryan, John Neely, 119
Bryan, William Joel, 49
Bryson, 175, 178
Bryson, Henry, 175
Buchanan, 132, 150
Buchanan, James, 150
Buck, Frank, 187, **187**
Buckholts, 45
Buckholts, John, 46
Buckner, Aylett C., 17, 18
Buckner's Creek, 17
Bucksnort, 107
Buescher State Park, 34
Buffalo Springs, 168, **168**
Burdick, Dick, 34
Burkburnett, 164, 165, **165**, 166
Burkburnett boom, 165, 166
Burleson, 133, 134

Burleson County, 38-42
Burleson County Historical Society, 39
Burleson County Museum, 42
Burleson, Edward, 41, 135
Burleson house, Smithville, 32, **32**
Burleson, Rufus, 74, 75, 135
Burlington, 183
Burnam's Ferry, 9
Burnett, Samuel Burk, 165
Burr, Aaron, 2
Burton gin, 67, **67**
Burton, John, 67
Bustamente, Anastacio, 4
Butler, 32
Butterfield Overland Mail, 123, 161, 171, 180, 187
Butterfield Road, 176
Byars, Noah, 61
Bybee, Mr. and Mrs. Charles, 22
Byers, 168

C

Caddo, 151
Caddo Indians, 101, 106, 110, 173, 190
Caldwell, 38-41
Caldwell County, 25-29
Caldwell County Courthouse, 26
Caldwell County Museum, 26, **26**
Caldwell, Matthew, 20, 25, 41
Call Field marker, 164, **164**
Call, Loren, 166
Callisburg, 188
Calvert, 103, 105, **105**, 106
Calvert, Robert, 105
Cambridge, 167, 168
Cameron, 45, 46
Cameron, Ewen, 45
Cameron house, Waco, 76, **76**
Cameron, William, 76
Camp Bowie, 87, 88, 127
Camp Cooper, 173
Camp Henderson, 133
Camp Hood, 80, 114
Camp Howze, 189

Manheim, 34
Mann, John W., 75
Mansker, William, 146
Marcy, Randolph, 184
Margaret Houston house, 63, **63**
Maria, Jose, 108
Marlin, 107, 108, **108**
Marlin, John, 107, 108
Martin, Mary, 156
Martindale, 27
Martindale, Nancy, 27
Mary Hardin Baylor University, 75, 112, **112**
Matagorda Bay, 51
Maximillian, 14
Maxwell, 27
Maxwell, Thomas, 27
May, 87
Mayeye Indinas, 42
Meichinger, Martin, 87
Mercer, Peter, 61
Meridian, 92, 93
Meridian State Recreation Area, 93, **93**
Merriman, 146
Mesquiteville, 175
Mexia, 100, 101
Mexia, Jorge, 100
Mexia Oil Field, 100, 101, **101**
Mier Expedition, 45, 62
Milam, Ben, 42, 43
Milam County, 42-46
Milam County Courthouse, 42, **42**
Milam County Museum, 43, **43**
Milano, 46
Miller mill, Dublin, 144, **144**
Millican, 49
Millican, Elliott and Robert, 48
Milligan gin, 13
Milligan, William, 13
Milliken, Sam, 142
Mills County, 83-85
Mills County Historical Museum, 84
Mills County Jail, 84, **84**
Mills, John T., 84
Mina, Francisco Xavier, 31

Mineral baths, Marlin, 109
Mineral Wells, 152-154
Mineral Wells baths, 153, **153**
Mingus, 154
Mississippi River, 51
Missouri, Kansas & Texas Railroad, 59, 75, 97, 114
Mobley Hotel, Cisco, 148, **148**
Moccasin Belle (boat), 13
Modern Art Museum of Fort Worth, 127, **127**
Monastery of St. Clare, 66, **66**
Monclova, 106
Montague County, 182-186
Montague County Courthouse, 184, **184**
Montague, Daniel, 185
Monument Hill, 17, **17**, 18, 21, 45
Moody, 77
Moody Drug Store, 77, **77**
Moody, W. L., 77
Moore, John Henry, 18
Moore, Sam and Will, 16
Morgan, 93, 105
Morgan, George, 108
Morgan Mill, 145
Mormon, 110
Morris Sheppard Dam, 175
Morton Museum, Gainesville, 190
Moss, Charlie and William, 136
Moss Lake, 189
Mother Neff State Park, 81
Moulton, 15-17
Mount Airy, 144
Mount Pleasant Cemetery, Franklin, 104
Muenster, 188
Mulberry, 25
Muldoon, 20
Muldoon, Michael, 20
Mullin, 83, 84
Mullin United Methodist Church, 84, **84**
Mullins, Mrs. J. L., 110
Municipality of Milam, 43, 79
Municipality of Mina, 30

206

Minicipality of Viesca, 43
Municipality of Washington, 56
Museum of Aviation, Fort Worth, 131
Museum of Natural History, New York, 136

N

Nails Creek Division, Lake Somerville State Park, 38
Napoleon, 1
Nashville, 43, 46
Nashville Colony, 102
Navarro, Jose Antonio, 40
Navasota, 52-54
Navasota River, 46, 48, 101
Navidad River, 13
Navy space antenna, 171, **171**
Nelsonville, 7, **7**
Neff, Pat, 72, 80, **80**, 101
Neighbors, Robert, 149, 172, 173
Nesterville, 165
Newcastle, 175
Ney, Elisabet, 56
Nocona, 184
Nocona Boot Co., 183, **183**
Nocona, Peta, 98
Nolan Creek, 113
Nolan, Philip, 2, 94, 135
Nolan River, 135
Nolan Springs, 112
Nolansville, 113
Northrup, 35
North Texas Normal College, 191
Norway Mill, 92
Norwegian settlements, 91, 92
Nuestra Senora de la Candelaria, 42
Nutt House, Granbury, 140, **140**
Nutt, J. F. and J., 141

O

Oakwood Cemetery, Waco, 72
Oil City, 168
"Old Rip", 147

Old San Antonio Road (Old Spanish Road, Camino Real), 27, 29, 34, 41, 46, 103
Olney, 174
Orcoquiza Indians, 42
Owensville, 103, 105

P

Paige, 32
Palo Alto, 114
Palo Pinto, 152, 154
Palo Pinto County, 152-154
Palo Pinto County Pioneer Museum, 152, **152**
Palo Pinto Creek, 152
Paluxy River, 136
Parilla, Diego Ortiz, 171, 182
Parker County, 154-159
Parker County Courthouse, 155, **155**
Parker, Cynthia Ann, 98, **98**, 157, 184
Parker, Isaac, 155, **155**, 157
Parker, James, Silas and John, 97, 98
Parker, Quanah, 98, 184
Pate, A. M., Jr., 155
Pate Museum of Transportation, 155, **155**
Payne, Howare, 86
Peace Party, 188
Peanuts, 147, **147**
Pecan Bayou, 86
Pecan Creek, 82
Pecan Valley Baptist Association, 86
Peebles, Richard, 56
Peerson, Cleng, 91, **91**
Perot, Ross, Jr., 123
Perry, H. G., 143
Peter Pan Statue, Weatherford, 156, **156**
Peters Colony, 120, 131, 190
Peters, W. S., 118, 190
Petersburg, 13
Petrolia, 168
Petrolia Field Marker, 166, **166**
Philen house, Hearne, 104, **104**

Picketville, 151
Pilot Point, 193
Pinckney, John, 59
Pinckneyville, 192
Pioneer Association of Denton County, 192
Pioneer Rest Cemetery, Fort Worth, 120, 122, **122**
Pioneer Village Museum, Lexington, 37
Planters' State Bank, 80
Plum Creek, 26
Plum Creek fight, 25, 27, **27**
Possum Kingdom Reservoir, 175
Possum Kingdom State Park, 154, **154**
Pottsville, 83
Powell, Peter, 17, 18
Praha, 25
Prairie Lea, 27, 28
Prairie View A & M University, 57, **57**, 58
Prairie View Plantation, 58
Presidio San Francisco Xavier, 42
Priddy, 84
Provisional Government of Texas, 4, 5

R

Rabb, William, 18
Rabbs Creek, 18
Raby Park, Gatesville, 79, **79**
Raccoon Bend, 8
Railroad and Pioneer Museum, Temple, 111, **111**
Ramirez y Sesma, 9
Ramon, Domingo, 25, 101
Ranger, 146, **146**, 148, 149
Ranger Camp Valley, 148
Ranger oil boom, 148, 149
Ratliff, John, 38
Reagan, 110
Rebago y Teran, Felipe, 42

Red Gap, 146
Red River Station, 183
Regency suspension bridge, 85, **85**
Reno, 157
Richardson, Israel, 176
Richardson, Sid, 129
Riemenschneider's Furniture Store, 15
Ringgold, 183, 185
Rio Vista, 131, 134
Rising Star, 148
Rivera, Pedro de, 25, 48
Roanoke, 193
Roberts, Brushy Bill, 83
Robertson Colony, 38, 43, 70, 78, 81, 83, 92, 102, 103, 106, 110, 131, 136
Robertson County, 101-106, 142
Robertson, Elijah Sterling C., 113
Robertson, Felix and Sterling, 43, 78, 101, 103, 106, 113
Robertson house, Salado, 113, **113**
Robertson, Sterling, 102, **102**
Robinson, Andrew, 59
Robnett, J. D., 86
Robson Castle, 12
Robson, Robert, 12
Rockdale, 45
Roitsch, Mr. and Mrs. Edgar, 20, **20**
Roosevelt, Franklin D., 154
Roosevelt, Theodore, 165
Rosanky, 32, 34
Rosanky, Ed, 32
Rosebud, 110
Ross, Lawrence Sullivan, 48, 72, 74
Ross, Shapley Prince, 74
Rosston Store, 189, **189**
Round Rock, 193
Round Top, 22
Round Top Community Center, 22, **22**
Ruiz, Jose Francisco, 38-40
Runaway Scrape, 107
Ruter College, 21
Ruter, Martin, 21
Rutersville, 21

S

St. Helen, John, 138, 141
St. James Episcopal Church, La Grange, 19, **19**
Saint Jo, 183-185
Saint Jo Saloon Museum, 184, **184**
St. Louis & Southwestern Railroad, 95
St. Mary's Church, Praha, 25, **25**
St. Mary's Church, Windthorst, 169, **169**
St. Olaf's Lutheran Church, 92, **92**
St. Paul's Lutheran Church, Serbin, 35, **35**
Salado, 113
Salado College, 113, 114, **114**
Salado Creek, 113
Salado Creek battle, 20, 26
Salt Creek, 175
Salt Hill, 175
Saltillo, 102, 106
San Antonio & Aransas Pass Railroad, 15, 17, 110
San Felipe Church, 4, **4**
San Felipe de Austin, 2, 4, 5, 6, 9
San Felipe Town Hall, 3, **3**
San Francisco Xavier de Horcasits, 42
San Gabriel River, 42
San Ildefonso, 42
San Jacinto, 6, 9
San Jacinto Hotel, Weimar, 12, **12**
San Marcos River, 28
San Saba Mission, 182
San Xavier Missions, 42
Sanchez, Frank, 146
Sandefer, J. D., 150
Sanders-Metzger Gun Collection, A & M, 51
Santa Anna, Antonio Lopez de, 4, 5, 6, 9, 27, 45
Santa Fe depot, Fort Worth, 130, **130**
Santa Fe depot, Gainesville, 189, **189**
Santa Fe depot, Weatherford, 155, **155**
Santa Fe Expedition, 25, 62
Santa Fe Railroad, 93, 111

Sarahville de Viesca, 106, 107
Satank, 176, 177
Santana, 176, 177
Sayers house, Bastrop, 30, **30**
Sayers, Joseph D., 30
Schulenburg, 21
Schulenburg, Louis, 21
Scott, A. C., 114
Scott, J. A., 162
Scott-White Hospital, 111, **111**, 114
Seagrams, 149
Sealy, 12
Sebesta's Corner, 41
Secessionist vigilantes, 125
Second Armored Division, 80-115
Seidel, William, 67
Senftenburg-Brandon house, Columbus, 10, **10**
Serbin, 35
Seventh Day Adventists, 133
Shaw, James, 34
Shawnee Indians, 190
Sheppard Air Force Base, 164, **164**
Sheppard, Morris, 164
Sherman, William T., 174, 176, 177, **177**, 178
Shiner, 15
Shiner, H. B., 15
Shinoak, 148
Shive, 83
Shoup, Mike, 64
Shuffler, Henderson, 32
Sipe Springs, 90
Sironia, Texas (novel), 76
Six Flags Over Texas, 119, **119**
Six Shooter, 27
Six Shooter Junction, 59
Skidmore, Elijah, 171
Slaughter, Christopher Columbus, 152
Slaughter, Gene and Frankie, 63
Slaughter, George Webb, 152
Slaughter, John B. and Will B., 152
Slavery, 57
Smith, Frank, 32
Smith, Lee, 48

Texas College of Osteopathic Medicine, 128
Texas Declaration of Independence, 2, 4, 5, 25, 40, 41, 52, 61, 64, 67, 105
Texas Department of Agriculture, 20, 37, **37**
Texas Department of Corrections, 80
Texas Folklore Society, 93
Texas Monumental and Military Institute, 21
Texas Pacific Coal Company, 145, 148
Texas Pacific Coal and Oil Company, 145, 149
Texas & Pacific Railroad, 125, 146, 148, 157
Texas Pioneer Arts Foundation, 22
Texas Railroad Commission, 144
Texas Ranger Hall of Fame and Museum, 71, **71**
Texas Rangers, 3, 70, 71, 98, 101, 186, 193
Texas Safari Wildlife Park, 91, **91**
Texas Transportation Institue, 50, **50**
Texas Union Baptist Association, 65
Texas Weslayan College, 128
Texas Woman's University, 191, 192
Texas Youth Council, 80
The Grove, 80, **80**
The Iconoclast, 72
"The Last Picture Show," 170
The Whiteman, 176
Thirty-sixth Divison, 127
Thirty-sixth Division Memorial Park, 87, **87**
Thistle Hill, Fort Worth, 130, **130**
Thomas, Speedy, 28, **28**
Thorndale, 45
Thornton, 100
Thorp, Pleasant, 139, 142
Thorp Spring, 139
Thorp Spring Christian College, 141
Three D brand, 165
Thurber, 145

Tonkawa Indians, 29, 34, 70, 136, 146, 173
Top of the Hill Terrace, 121
Torrey Trading Co., 70, 71, 73, 136
Traders' Village, Grand Prairie, 120, **120**
Trading Post and Old West Museum, 185
Travis, William Barret, 27, 175
Trigg, Edna Westbrook, 44, **44**
Trinity & Brazos Valley Railroad, 100
Trinity Lutheran Church, Frelsburg, 11, **11**
Trinity River, 122
Trinity University, 99
Troy, 89
"Twin Sisters" (cannons), 58

U

United Daughters of the Confederacy Museum, 9, **9**
University of North Texas, 191, **191**, 192
University of Texas at Arlington, 119, **119**, 128
Urschel, Charles, 181

V

Valley Mills, 93
Van Bibber, Mr. ad Mrs. Dion, 114
Vaughn, Reuben, 152
Velasco, 18
Viesca, Agustin, 106

W

Waco, 69-78
Waco Art Cetner, 76, **76**
Waco Council Grounds, 73
Waco Indians, 69-71, 101, 106, 173
Waco & Northwest Railroad, 110
Waco tornado (1953), 75
Waco University, 65, 74
Waggoner, Dan, 154, 156, 164, 180
Waggoner house, Decatur, 180, **180**
Waggoner Ranch, 180, 181
Waggoner, W. T., 164

Walker house, Brownwood, 86, **86**
Walker, Sam, 27
Waller, 58
Waller County, 56-59
Waller County Historical Museum, 58, **58**
Waller, Edwin, 58
Walnut Springs, 93
Wantke, John, 22
Ward, William, 132
Wardville, 132
Warren, Henry, 174, 176
Washington County, 5, 59-67
Washington-on-the-Brazos, 2, 5, 59, 60, 61, 62, 64
Watermelons, 59, **59**, 159
Waterworks Restaurant, Waco, 76, **76**
WBAP-TV, 125, **125**
Weatherford College, 153
Weatherford, Jefferson, 157
Weaver Apiary, 53, **53**
Weimar Country Inn, 12, **12**
Wendish Heritage Museum, 38
Wesley Brethren Church, 67, **67**
Westminister College, 99, **99**
Westphalia, 110
Wheeler Creek, 136
Wheelock, 105
White, R. R., 114
Whitney, 94, 95
Whyte, Edna Gardner, 193, **193**
Wichita County, 162-166
Wichita Falls, 162-164, 166
Wichita Falls Museum and Art Center, 161, **161**, 162
Wichita Falls & Northwestn Railroad, 165
Wichita Indians, 162
Wichita River, 162
Wichita Valley Railroad, 168
Wilbarger, Josiah, 29, 30
Wildflower seed farm, 11

Williams, John, 83
Williams Ranch Settlement, 83-85, **85**
Williams, Samuel M., 105, 146
Williams, Walter, 104, **104**
Williamson, R. M., 10
Willow Springs, 77
Will Rogers Coliseum, 118, **118**
Winchester, 17
Windthorst, 169
Windthorst, Ludwig, 170
Winedale Historic Center, 24, **24**
Wise County, 178-182
Wise County Courthouse, 179, **179**
Wise County Heritage Museum, 181, **181**
Wise, Henry A., 178
Wizard Wells, 178
Woll, Adrian, 20, 25
Wolters, Jacob F., 154
Woody cabin, Wise County, 179, **179**
Woody, Sam, 178
Worth, William Jenkins, 121, **121**, 122
WPA, 154, 176
Wren, Josephine, 133

X

Xarame Indians, 59

Y

Yellow fever, 63
Yoakum, 15
Yoakum, B. F., 15
Young County, 171-175
Young County Courthouse, 173, **173**

Z

Zedler, Fritz, 28
Zedler Mill, Luling, 28, **28**
Zwiener, Doug, 64